Praise for the Dating Goddess

The *Adventures in Delicious Dating After 40* series of books is based on the blog Adventures in Delicious Dating After 40 at www.DatingGoddess.com. Here are comments from readers.

♥ "Adventures in Delicious Dating After 40 is a wonderful composite of both the mechanics of post-40 online dating and what the practice of honoring one's self actually looks like. How marvelous your writing is to read. I spent about 2 hours reading and was riveted the whole time." —Maggie Hanna

♥ "At last, a dating writer who addresses requirements. You are SO right on! I'm thrilled to have found you!" —Rachel Sarah, author, *Single Mom Seeking*

♥ "Powerfully heartfelt and honest writing. You are inspiring." —Kare Anderson, Emmy Award winning writer

"I just love your writing. It is very fresh and gives the reader something to think about." —Kelly Lantz, President & Manager, 55-Alive.com

"Dating Goddess, you are like a, a, a, well, a goddess to me. You've helped guide me successfully through my re-entry into the dating world after 14 years. I'm an eager student and fast study, and do get myself into situations that others don't know how to deal with — such as 3 dates in one day -— so thankfully you are there! You're the greatest, thanks for all you do for us!" —Jae G.

"I find your point of view much more interesting than other dating writers. Thanks for always reminding me to enjoy dating life no matter what it throws at you." —Sandy

"I love Adventures in Delicious Dating After 40. I really do like your honest and authentic voice — it's refreshing." —Wendy S.

"Adventures in Delicious Dating After 40 is really fun to read. Thanks for sharing your thoughts and letting us divorced single women know that we are not alone. There's a lot here that I identify with, although I'm not as brave as you are about dating lots of guys. So far. Love your blog — the first blog I've ever read consistently." —Elizabeth

"Thanks for a wonderful blog. You're doing a great job of saying what's in my mind. There's rarely a day I miss when it comes to checking in on your wisdom." —Paulette Ensign

Assessing Your Assets

Why You're A Great Catch

by **Dating Goddess**

Assessing Your Assets: Why You're A Great Catch

Second Edition

Cover design by Dave Innis, www.innisanimation.com

Book design by JustYourType.biz

Printed in the United States of America.

ISBN   print: 978-1-930039-34-6

eBook: 978-1-930039-12-4

How to order:

The *Adventures in Delicious Daing After 40* books may be ordered directly from www.DatingGoddess.com.

Quantity discounts are also available. Visit us online for updates and additional articles.

The Adventures in Delicious Dating After 40 books are dedicated to my ex-husband since he unexpectedly released me to explore the untethered life of a single woman. I then had the freedom for the experiences, lessons and insights shared in these pages.

Books by Dating Goddess

💜 Date or Wait: Are You Ready for Mr. Great?

💜 Assessing Your Assets: Why You're A Great Catch

💜 In Search of King Charming: Who Do I Want to Share My Throne?

💜 Embracing Midlife Men: Insights Into Curious Behaviors

💜 Dipping Your Toe in the Dating Pool: Dive In Without Belly Flopping

💜 Winning at the Online Dating Game: Stack the Deck in Your Favor

💜 Check Him Out Before Going Out: Avoiding Dud Dates

💜 First-Rate First Dates: Increasing the Chances of a Second Date

💜 Real Deal or Faux Beau: Should You Keep Seeing Him?

💜 Multidating Responsibly: Play the Field Without Being A Player

💜 Moving On Gracefully: Break Up Without Heartache

💜 From Fear to Frolic: Get Naked Without Getting Embarrassed

💜 Ironing Out Dating Wrinkles: Work Through Challenges Without Getting Steamed

Contents

Introduction

This book is designed for anyone who is interested in stories, advice, and lessons from the midlife dating front. If you are over 40 and haven't dated in a while — or even if you have — you'll learn ways to approach dating with zeal, optimism, and hope. Even if you've had more than your share of negative experiences, I'll share how to glean lessons from those adventures, rather than just declaring that "all men are jerks" or "men are just looking for sex."

While most of the perspective is from a woman to women, men's comments, experiences, and lessons have been integrated as appropriate.

This book began as daily entries into my blog, Adventures in Delicious Dating After 40, which has been featured in the *Wall Street Journal* as well as radio and TV. I wrote about my epiphanies from my and my friends' dating life. The best postings were culled to make this and subsequent books.

This book focuses on helping you look at your why you are such a great catch. Women often discount their attributes. This book will help you see your good points so you'll approach dating with more confidence.

This book consists of three types of perspectives:

Lessons: These are specific experiences I thought would be useful to you. A few lines from my experience illustrate the points.

Insights: These usually start with an experience I've encountered, then the insights that experience spawned. It is usually comprised of around half story and half insight.

Stories: These are examples of situations I've experienced — or was currently experiencing when I wrote that piece — that I thought would be entertaining. Or I thought the story would help you see what kind of things happen in the midlife dating world so you'd know what has happened to others.

Because these writings were real time, as they occured, they are often set in the present tense. But they are not chronological. So a reference to "my current beau" may now be many sweethearts ago. I hope this isn't confusing.

I'd love ot hear your stories and questions. Please email them to me at Goddess@DatingGoddess.com. They may make it into the blog or my next book!

Who is the Dating Goddess?

I am a middle-aged, white, professional woman. My husband of nearly 20 years left me in April 2003 when I was 47, 11 days shy of 48. After giving my heart time to heal from the surprise divorce sprung by the man I thought was my soulmate, I started dating 18 months later. Generally, I have had a great time meeting interesting men, some of whom became romantic beaus, some became treasured friends, and some I never heard from again.

I am not a well-preserved, gorgeous, marathon-running middle-aged women

In the beginning, I had dates with single male colleagues, but I quickly found Internet dating was the way to explore the most "inventory" and qualify men who I thought might be a good match.

I am not one of those well-preserved, gorgeous,

marathon-running middle-aged women. I have been told I am attractive, but I am overweight and not a gym rat. So while I am active, I do not match the description 90% of men's profiles say they want: slender, athletic, toned, fit. I have some wrinkles — what one sweet suitor mistakenly called dimples. I have what Bridget Jones called "wobbly bits," as most non-surgically enhanced middle-aged women do. My genes — and a lifetime addiction to chocolate — have made their mark. Yet I've met and dated some wonderful men, so even if you're not a lingerie model, you can find guys who will think you're attractive, perhaps even hot!

In my professional life, I am a bestselling author of workplace effectiveness books, professional speaker and management consultant. I've appeared on Oprah, 60 Minutes, and National Public Radio and in the *Wall Street Journal* and *USA Today.*

This book is intended to not only be useful to others and cathartic for me, but is also the genesis of a new topic for fun, thought-provoking speeches. I'm calling myself a dating philosopher and giving date-a-vational speeches! Let me know if you know a group who would like an entertaining after-lunch speech on how lessons learned from dating have implications in business and personal relationships and well as life philosophies.

How did I come by the Dating Goddess moniker? After a few months of dating dozens of men — one week yielded 7 dates with 6 guys in 5 days — my friends dubbed me this name. I liked it, so it stuck.

I'm purposefully not sharing my picture as I don't want you to think either, "How did she get any dates at all?" or the opposite, "Of course she found it easy to get 112 men to ask her out." I am not hideous (usually) nor am I stunning (without professional hair, makeup and Photoshop!). Some men find me attractive, some don't.

I continue to search for my "one," but I have learned a lot along the way, and my single and not-single friends have loudly encouraged me to share my experiences and lessons in the hopes of helping others navigate the adventure of dating with more success. And to have a delicious time doing it!

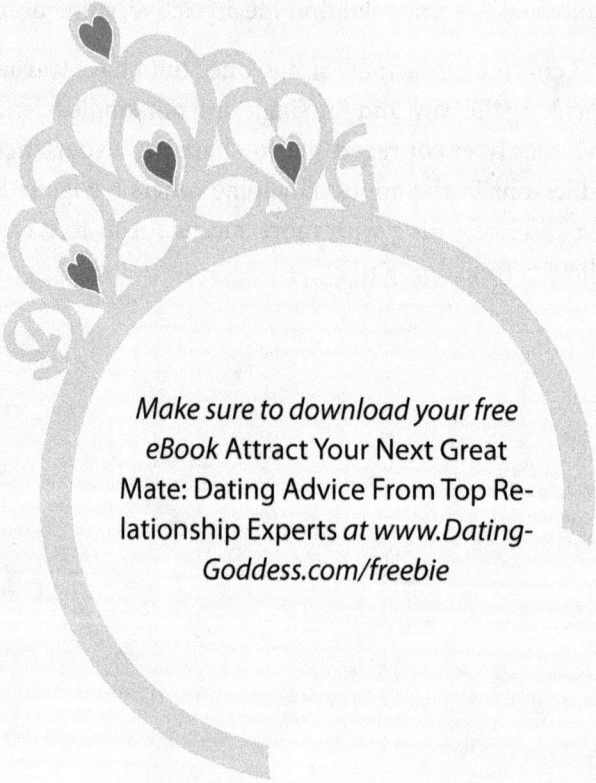

Make sure to download your free eBook Attract Your Next Great Mate: Dating Advice From Top Relationship Experts *at www.Dating-Goddess.com/freebie*

Don't think you are damaged goods

When you reenter the dating world in midlife, it is easy to focus on what is wrong with you. Your body is not as firm and lithe as it was in your 20's. You have wrinkles, perhaps cellulite, maybe some gray hair. You probably don't have as much energy as you used to, or you have physical limitations due to injuries or parts wearing down. You might have kids living at home and feel few men would want to deal with that.

Men seem to be most concerned about their hair loss. Women seem most concerned about weight gain. I've learned that many men are less concerned about a woman's few extra pounds; women are less concerned about a man's receding hairline.

You should never feel as if you are damaged goods. If you are having self-doubts, make a list (maybe with the aid of a good friend) of all your positive characteristics. You want to exude confidence (without arrogance) so a man knows he is lucky to spend time with you.

If you feel you could update your image, go to the makeup counter at one of the major department stores and have a makeover. It's typically free. Buy some of the makeup and wear it when you go out, even to the grocery store. You never know if you'll run into your next husband in the cat food aisle, as one of my friends did.

Also, Macy's and Nordstrom have personal shoppers that can help you update your look. There is no cost for the service. Call and make an appointment. Tell her you're looking for some dating clothes, give her your size and colors, and when you arrive she will have pulled items for you to try. I've used these services many, many times. You aren't obligated to buy anything, and she will bring you sale items as well as full-priced ones. She will help put together the whole outfit, including shoes, hose, and accessories so you feel totally pulled together.

If you're out of shape, start walking even if it's only 15 minutes a day. It will do wonders for your outlook on life, and it will begin to tone things up. If you are more energetic, take an exercise class. It's amazing how quickly your energy and body can change.

So there is no excuse for you to feel that you are less than stellar. You want to put your best foot forward on each date, so do what you need to do to accomplish that.

What do you need to do to get ready for dating? Put your plan into action this week.

You are (probably) more attractive than you think!

It seems that people have a mismatch on their expectation of attractiveness. The stereotype is that a man wants (and often gets) a woman who is much more attractive than he is. Women often put money, status, demeanor and sense of humor ahead of attractiveness, when looks are often at or near the top of the "must haves" for men.

In college I duplicated a study matching couples by attractiveness. I took the pictures of 10 long-term couples from my high-school yearbook and had subjects rate the attractiveness of all 20 people individually. Then I had them match people who seemed to go together. While few people found the true couples, they did match approximate attractiveness levels. So those rated 8-10 (10 being high) were put together, as were the 5-7s, 4-6s, etc.

So why do men who would be rated a 6 seem to think

they can get a woman who's an 8? They think they're "all that" when really they're so so. Because the woman only thinks she's a 5, 6, or 7.

In a recent study, school children were asked what level of student they were. The girls consistently rated themselves lower than their average performance; the boys rated themselves higher. An A-student girl said she was a B or B+ student. A B-student boy said he was an A student. So girls and boys have a skewed image of themselves, with boys thinking more highly of themselves than warranted, and girls thinking lower of themselves.

Girls and boys have a skewed image of themselves

So women (generally) think they aren't as attractive or as desirable as independent raters would assess them.

How would you rate yourself? Whatever the number, bump it a bit. You're no doubt a better catch than you think yourself to be!

The downside of considering yourself pretty

Most of the women I know underestimate their attractiveness, not overestimate it. It is easy to be acutely aware of each of your "flaws" since you examine millimeters of your face and body every day — sometimes at 5x magnification. I am astounded when I hear top models complaining about a crooked nose, uneven skin tone or wrinkles no one else would see.

But there are women who consider themselves hot, stunning, and/or breathtaking. Such vanity can either be a sign of true high self-esteem, focusing on only one's positive attributes. Or it can be an outward showing of low self-esteem — if one believes herself ugly but thinks that pretending to be beautiful will make others believe so. Sort of like the Emperor's New Clothes — if you project it, others will believe it.

Unusually high self-regard can be detrimental. In the 1722 novel by Daniel Defoe The Fortunes and Misfortunes of the Famous Moll Flanders, the title character says that those who think of themselves as beautiful are easier to seduce: "If a young woman once thinks herself handsome, she never doubts the truth of any man that tells her he is in love with her; for she believes herself charming enough to captivate him, 'tis natural to expect the effects of it."

So are women who consider themselves beautiful more vulnerable to manipulation? Are they prone to believe any man who tells them they are beautiful because, well, they are? So they think they have beguiled a man, when he may just be saying that or it may be for a momentary seduction.

We could argue that a woman who doesn't consider herself attractive is more vulnerable as she can be manipulated by a man who tells her she is beautiful. She may not hear compliments as often so feels he must be sincere.

What do you think — is it easier to be manipulated if you think you are beautiful or unattractive?

A related piece, "Why men don't tell you you're pretty" is in the *Embracing Midlife Men: Insights Into Curious Behaviors* book.

They aren't called "hate handles"

Many midlife woman have bodies with a bit more to love than they did in their twenties. Some are self-conscious about their less-than-model-like shapes. I have been.

But then a few men have helped me see that pronounced curves have admirers. When discussing our body images with one beau, I shared that I wasn't happy with my generous hips. His reply: "I love your hips. You know, they aren't called 'hate handles.'" Of course, I kissed him right then and there.

Another commented that my considerable tush should "be proclaimed a national treasure." Now you've got to just love a man who says things like that!

Pronounced curves have admirers

I was reminded of these sweet-talking endearments upon hearing a

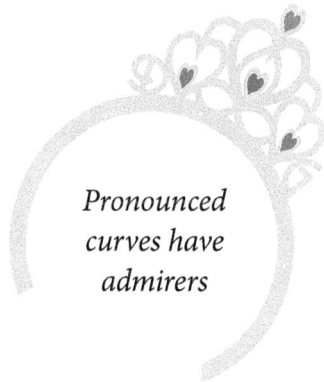

comment by Guy Ritchie after his and Madonna's divorce announcement. I've long admired her lithe, chiseled body. But evidently he did not. During their estrangement, he was quoted saying that making love to Madonna was like "having sex with gristle."

The point is that there are men who love all body types. And what may seem attractive to you in other women, may not be at all attractive to many men. We need to embrace who we are and appreciate whatever we bring to the party, knowing there are some men who will love us for — or despite — whatever part of ourselves we may not fully love.

"I could really see us together if you lost weight"

Most of us would be incensed hearing this. I wasn't. A dear male pal, someone I'd dated briefly 18 months ago, told me this recently. We were having a heart to heart, honest talk about the ups and downs of dating and why I hadn't found Mr. Right yet.

About a month after our first date, we decided we weren't a good match, but we still enjoyed each others' company. We've kept in touch regularly, seeing each other monthly and talking weekly. While he thinks I'm pretty and sexy, my body type is not the kind that turns him on. And as much as I adore him as a pal, he has some quirks that would drive me crazy if he was my man.

What if someone who really interested you said this? Would you be crushed, incensed, or step up your efforts to lose some lingering extra pounds? Both genders long for someone who will love us exactly the way we are. Yet it is commonly acknowledged that women often see a man as a project, wanting to change his wardrobe, job, car, friends, furnishings, hair cut, etc. How is this different than a man wanting us to sculpt our body closer to what he desires?

Today I heard Ruben Studdard singing "Change Me." In it, he asks his woman how would she feel if he complained about her hair, nail polish color, clothes, friends, job, cooking, housekeeping, etc. His point is that she wouldn't like it, so why does she think he will put up with her constant complaints about him? The chorus, "Why do you want to change me?" echoes what men and women have felt for ages.

You have to decide what the deal breakers are for you. And if there are things you'd like him to change, consider how easy they are to change. And how important are they to him? What if he really likes his job, but you think he doesn't make enough money? Can you live with it, or are you willing to figure out how you both could create more income for both of you without his changing jobs? Or is it a deal breaker?

Better identify your deal breakers while early in the dating cycle lest you try to change a deal breaker that he is unwilling to modify — after you've invested months in the relationship. And what would you be willing to change for someone you cared about?

"I only want to date someone I would marry"

A newly divorced friend was clear my philosophy about dating many men wouldn't work for her. She said, "I just couldn't do that. I don't want to date anyone I wouldn't see myself marrying."

She is not alone. This is many women's philosophy. She says she is too busy to spend time with someone she doesn't think she might marry.

I understand her point of view. Dating takes time. I, too, have cut off dating someone I knew wasn't a match. It wouldn't be fair to him to lead him on.

On the other hand, I've had dates with men who I wasn't sure were a match or not. Sometimes you know on the first date it's not a match. But sometimes you don't know until after the second, third, or additional dates.

In fact, I've gone out with men who were a nanosecond away from receiving my "Thanks, but no thanks" message, but something compelled me to write a more thoughtful note. If he responded positively with why he thought we could be a good match, I might be convinced to continue the correspondence, perhaps progressing to a phone call and maybe an eventual date. Some of these nanosecond-away-from-being-deleted guys have turned out to be treasures as pals.

And some of those nearly deleted guys have ended up as beaus. I've found you just don't know if the connection is there until you meet someone. Although, sometimes you know in email or the phone if they are paranoid, sex-focused, foul-mouthed, angry, manipulative, self-focused, poor conversationalists or have other deal-breaking habits. Then there's no need to meet. But if all lights are green, why not meet and see if they stay green, or if yellow or red flashes?

A guy pal said he sometimes continued dating someone he knew wasn't a match because they liked some of the same activities. In his mind, someone, even a not-long-term match, was better than experiencing pastimes alone. This could be okay as long as you both agree you aren't a long-term match, and that your seeing each other casually doesn't slow down your search for a long-term mate.

Where do you stand on this? Do you only want to date someone you think has long-term potential? Or will you date more than a few times someone you know isn't a good match?

Are you a hoochie mama?

"What's that?" you ask.

The term is commonly used to denote a loose or crass woman. However, because I have a dear friend who uses this as an endearing term for me, I like to think of it differently. My definition is a woman who is secure in her sexuality, comfortable flirting and playing. She knows how to be sexy and suggestive and not cross over to bawdy, ribald, obscene, vulgar, crude, coarse, lewd, dirty, or smutty. I think of Mae West as the exemplar.

You are a hoochie mama if:

- You laugh at others' funny, suggestive (not vulgar) jokes.

- You occasionally make double entendres in private, to close friends or your lover.

- You find some of the cartoons in Playboy funny.

- You occasionally wear sexy clothing to appropriate events (not to work). You are not afraid to show cleavage or skin when it is appropriate for the function (e.g., cocktail party, formal event, beach).

♥ You are comfortable flirting with your dates and others who seem comfortable with it (not with your boss or his boss, or your best friend's husband if he seems uncomfortable).

You are not a hoochie mama if:

♥ You get offended when anyone makes any suggestive comment in a non-work setting. (I expect you to be offended if it is inappropriate, directed at you, at work, or raunchy).

A hoochie is a woman who is secure in her sexuality

♥ You feel it is inappropriate to exude any sexuality outside of your own home.

You have to decide for yourself if

♥ You are a hoochie mama, and

♥ If you aren't, do you want to be?

If the latter, how can you loosen up a bit without crossing the line to crassness?

You may wonder how I received the "Hoochie Mama" pet name from my friend. He and his wife live in New Orleans so right after my divorce they invited me to attend Mardi Gras with them. I did, and I came home with 50 pounds of beads. I had a great time. Since most people think there is only one way to get beads, if someone playful heard of my bead bounty, he'd look at me slyly. He'd say: "You must have done a lot of flashing to get all those beads."

So I created this hoochie-mama response: "There are various ways to earn beads. I won't share my secrets, but I will tell you to look for me in the next 'Middle-Aged Women Gone Wild' video. The good thing about being middle-aged is you don't have to raise your shirt very high to get beads." I smile and wink and move on. He usually laughs heartily.

Okay. Maybe I crossed the line.

A face perfect for radio

I'm sure you've heard that old insult. Well, after seeing myself on the Greg Behrendt Show, I feel I have a face perfect for radio. Or newspaper. Perhaps telegraph. Just not TV.

The producers invited me to appear on the show to ask a panel of celebrities some questions facing midlife dating women. Before the show Hollywood makeup and hair artists worked their magic on me. Still the sags and bags were pronounced. As I watched the tape, I wondered what man would ever agree to coffee, let alone a subsequent date. I pondered a second mortgage for a face lift.

Does this happen to you? You're lrammed up: full makeup, good hair day, a flattering frock. Someone snaps a pic. When you see it you think, "Who is that old/ chubby frump? And why is she wearing my outfit and sitting where I sat?"

Then it hits you: your self-image is different — sometimes very different — than how others see you. Sometimes this is a good thing, as it helps you have more confidence if you think you're looking good. And that poise, in fact, helps you appear more attractive.

Sometimes you feel you look worse than others see you. Your self-esteem doesn't match your outer appearance.

In dating, how you feel about yourself is sometimes affected by the reaction you get from your dates. If they continually shun you, you can begin to feel unappealing. And if you feel unattractive, no matter how many times your dates say you're beautiful, you won't believe them.

I've been lucky as I've had few men snub me. And even though when I smile the bags under my eyes grow gigantic, a smile is attractive on nearly everyone. But after seeing myself on camera, I wonder how any man could find my looks appealing. (I've seen myself on camera many times, but as one ages, the flaws are more distinct.)

My lesson: If you get a picture of yourself that is unflattering, don't linger on it. If you want to keep it as a memento of a special moment with people you love, great. If not, throw it away (or trim it and save the images you want in the pic). If there's an unbecoming video, just file it in the back of the closet.

However, if you look maaaaaavelous, put the photo where you can remind yourself you are appealing, especially after those dates where you got a chilly reception. Know that the man who is right for you will find you irresistible, and if a guy doesn't find you alluring, it's just not a match. Nothing personal. Next!

Are you a good man picker?

A pal lamented her string of dates who weren't a fit. She said, "I am struck by how consistently poor my 'picking ability' is."

How is your picking ability? Do you, too, have a string of first dates, but not second ones? Or you may have multiple dates, but nothing long term? After many go-nowhere first dates, I'm a pickier picker.

My grandmother was a cotton picker — she harvested cotton by hand on her family's farm as a young woman. (We loved telling her, "Take your cotton-picking hands off that!") She said there are ways to tell if the cotton is ready to be harvested.

If you're having a string of first dates and few second or third ones, let's apply some cotton-picking tips to man picking.

💜 Do you know what you're looking for? In cotton, you look for burst bolls (seed capsules). If you're not clear what you want, you'll go out with pretty much anyone. While I'm an advocate of meet-

ing men who don't meet your criteria 100%,
there are some who are just too far afield to be
a match. I now turn down 9 out of 10 inquiries
I receive. If you're not clear, read "What's your
"perfect boyfriend's" job description?" (see the
In Search of King Charming: Who Do I Want to
Share My Throne? book) and start writing yours.

Is he ready to be picked? If the bolls aren't open,
you can't harvest the cotton. If a man isn't ready
for a relationship, no matter what you do, he
won't do more than play around. Each man has
his own readiness signals, but working to please
you, talking about a future together and maturely discussing conflicts are good clues.

Are there indications this isn't a good pick?
Professional cotton farmers know crop problem signs. Although you're not a professional
dater, you know when you see insurmountable
problems. Don't ignore red flags. I don't agree to
meet with any man who uses foul language or
poor grammar in emails or on the phone. If he
doesn't seem to know how to make conversation,
dominates the discussion, or bashes his ex(es) or
women, I decline a face-to-face. (Read "First-date
red flags that this guy isn't for you" in First-Rate
First Dates: Increase the Chance of a Second Date.)

Additionally, do you establish some mutual
connection before meeting? If you go out with
someone after only a few brief contacts, you

don't know enough about him to know if he's a potential match. If you talk or email and ask some important questions, you're more likely to find someone who's going to be a fit. Don't interrogate him, but if his view on important issues is intolerable to you, there's not a match. Better know now than after spending more time exploring.

I believe every person I spend more than a few minutes with is a teacher. If you just dismiss the non-fits as cads, jerks or losers, you learn nothing. Why did you attract him to you? What is he there to teach you? If you don't learn the lesson, you'll keep getting more of the same until you do. So better sit down and ask yourself, "What did I learn from the encounter?" And saying, "Avoid losers" isn't an acceptable answer.

Even if you learned to better identify what you don't want, that's a good lesson. It will help you discern what you want and notice when a guy has it.

Sharpen your picking skills and you'll have better luck finding guys who are a better fit.

After many go-nowhere first dates, I'm a pickier picker.

Are you a good verbal hugger?

A verbal hug is a sincere acknowledgment. The usual result is that the receiver feels good. It's similar to a physical hug, but there's no touching — except the recipient's heart is often touched. You embrace him with your words. We all like sincere compliments, as long as it's not overdone.

A relationship is built upon positive experiences, as well as working through challenges with care. Verbal hugs help build a foundation with your man that shows you catch him doing things you like.

You can start giving verbal hugs in early emails and phone conversations and extend to face-to-face meetings. In emails, I try to find something in the guy's profile or previous emails that I admire and tell him so.

In a phone conversation it could be, "I'm glad we connected," "I'm glad you called," or "Thanks for giving me a call." At the end of a telephone conversation, instead of, "Talk to you later," try "It was really good to talk to you," or "I'm glad you called."

A relationship is built upon positive experiences

When meeting instead of asking the trite, "How are you?" try, "It's so good finally get to meet you," or, if it's true, "You look great." As he shares things you think are interesting or impressive, tell him so. Make a point to tell your date one thing you admire about him, "I admire how you have such patience with challenging people." Or reinforce a success with, "I applaud your fortitude to get your degree while raising a family."

However, don't pile it on too thick or it will seem that you're coming on too strong. See how he reacts. If he seems comfortable and also offers positive comments to you, you can continue to sprinkle your verbal hugs into conversations.

How can you "hug" your next date?

Walking over hot coals

W hen we say or hear, "I'd walk over hot coals to…" it shows unwavering commitment. Most of us would love it if a man said he'd walk over hot coals for our kiss!

Well, I've walked over a bed of hot coals — but it wasn't for a man. It was for me. I wasn't forced to do it. I did it to explode my self-imposed limits. And by doing so, it helped me become the person who can date with enthusiasm and less fear and a woman who my next mate will find irresistible.

When I met my ex I was 28. When we married I was 30. We often talked about how if we'd met five years earlier, neither of us would be the person the other would find attractive on an emotional and spiritual level. We hadn't yet grown into the individuals the other would fall in love with. We had baggage to jettison, anger to release, hearts to open. The five years before we met we each grew so we were ready when we did meet.

When I enrolled in the fire-walking seminar, I knew

no one would force me to walk over 12 feet of red-hot coals. Before the seminar, I convinced myself that I was enough of a risk taker that I didn't really have to walk on the coals. Up to moments before, I was sure I wouldn't do it. But I had an epiphany that if I didn't walk the coals, I'd be missing an opportunity to break through some limiting beliefs. With coaching from the staff, I safely walked. The exuberance I felt on the other side was something I've rarely experienced.

When I became single, I knew no one would force me to walk into the dating world, rife with potential heartbreak and pain. I was afraid to get started. A few dating friends gave me some tips, but my friend Caterina Rando convinced me to start walking the dating path by posting a profile. I had to face my fears with every early potential suitors' email, phone call and initial coffee date. The first time there was a mutual attraction, I was elated.

Are you the person your ideal mate would want to date? Have you worked through any anger, hurt or bitterness from past relationships? Have you resolved any issues around fear of intimacy and trust? Are you convinced you're a woman your man would be thrilled to meet, date and fall for?

Is there anything you need to work through so your heart will be open to your man? Are you willing to walk over your equivalent of hot coals to get to the you that you love without reservation so he will too? If not, what do you need to do to lose your own baggage?

Dating as therapy

Dating books say that dating shouldn't be used as therapy. In other words, you shouldn't use your guy to be your sounding board and work through issues as you would with a therapist. In fact, even if he is a therapist — *especially* if he is a therapist — you shouldn't expect him to act like he is your therapist.

That said, I've found dating can be good therapy. Some experiences have prompted me to look inward into why I did — or didn't — do something, or why I was drawn to a guy.

As fate would have it, I dated a psychiatrist for a while. After the initial few dates, I found him to be controlling and verbally abusive. I stuck with him longer than normal because I saw that his behavior paralleled a relative's. He was equally as incongruent, sometimes being loving, then moments later saying something to put me down. But I found it cathartic to say to him what I could never say to my relative: "You can't talk to me that way" and "You need to leave now because treating me that way is unacceptable." I'd tried role playing with various therapists saying things like this to my relative, and nothing ever shifted. But saying them to the crazy psychiatrist was liberating and healing.

I was not acting like he was my therapist, as his being a psychiatrist was inconsequential. In fact, when he encouraged me to work out with him the issues that he triggered, he got defensive and was a horrible listener.

Other times I'd look at why something bothered me. I was especially attracted to one man and he expressed equal attraction to me. Based on our discussions during our few dates, I thought we had a chance at something long-term. But he rarely called, although when we did talk he said he wanted to see me. I felt neglected during the week — or more — in between calls. He said I was welcome to call him if I wanted to talk. I did a few times, but it felt like I was chasing him when he didn't reciprocate initiating calls.

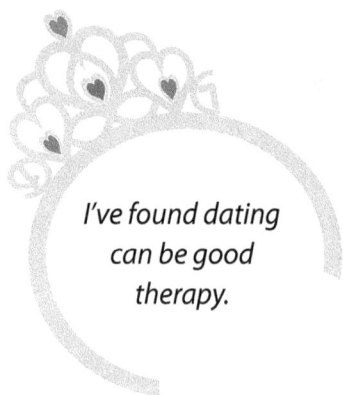

I've found dating can be good therapy.

This spawned a look at why daily calls are important to me with a romantic partner. I realized that when my ex left and said, "I don't think about you when you're not in the room" it seared a wound in my heart. I decided I deserved a man who thought about me when I wasn't in his presence. How would I know he did? He'd call and/or email at least once a day.

When I saw that this man wasn't filling my need, even when I told him about it, I understood that he and I weren't in a relationship, and apparently he had no desire to be in one with me. I loosened the daily contact requirement to every other day if it was a hardship for him, but even that didn't happen. So my gift from him was the trigger to go inside and figure out what was important to me and why. And to communicate it early with someone who seems a prospective long-term beau.

So you can use dating as a way to go deeper inside and to work through some issues. Best to do this with a trained therapist unless you feel comfortable doing the work with yourself.

Do you tend to your relationships the same as your plants?

While visiting a guy I was dating, I had some free time as he was BBQing dinner. I noticed some of his patio plants needed a little cleaning up. I asked him if I could tend to them and he said sure.

As I began to clean out the spent blooms and dried leaves, it struck me that perhaps how one cares for one's plants reflects how one cares for one's relationship(s). Noticing his plants were a little neglected, I wondered if that was what was in store for me.

Then I reflected on how I tend my own plants and what parallels I might draw. I purposefully have low-maintenance plants, both inside and outside. A year after my husband left, I decided I wanted front and back yards that gave me much joy and pleasure, but with little maintenance. Interesting that this decision was made within a few months of my beginning to date — to look for a man who I loved being with and gave me great joy — and, of course, pleasure! I merrily ripped out every shred of my dreary, married-life less-than-thriving front yard. Hmm, although I didn't admit it at the time, in retrospect, that is somewhat parallel to my near-the-end marriage.

Although it was hard work, I and a helper carefully and lovingly installed the new year-round blooming plants — and no lawn. Lawn would require mowing. Too much work! I wanted something joyful every season. My landscape designer even included a heart-shaped path. How serendipitous a meta-phor is that? We put in hard work to create a flourishing garden — isn't that part of any good relationship?

I don't want to have to take care of anything

Low maintenance was key for me. I installed an au-tomatically timed drip system so I didn't have to worry about watering. My ex liked to hand water the old yard. But he'd neglect to water and the plants showed it by staying small, ragged, or, ultimately, shriveling. Hmm, another apt parallel.

When friends would suggest I add a fountain, bird feeder or bird bath to my new yard, I'd quickly respond "I don't want to have to take care of anything." Since my ex was high maintenance — I did 90% of the "couples" business (paying bills, making travel plans, suggesting outings, household maintenance management), I am burnt out on taking care of things. I certainly don't want a man I have to take care of, and it would be nice for a change if he did a little taking care of me.

Recently I completed my yard overhaul by revamping my back yard, including taking out trees, lawn and some ratty old raised beds. I added a flagstone patio, several seating areas to enjoy the sun or shade, and all year-round blooming flowers. The flagstone is more permanent — reflecting, perhaps my desire and readiness for a more permanent relationship? We'll see. I do know I now love both my yards — and I will put the same thought and care into designing and nurturing my next relationship.

What are your deal breakers?

I was interviewed the other day by an engaging reporter from the San José Mercury News who was doing a piece on deal breakers. After over an hour on the phone, we'd explored this topic from nearly every angle.

He wanted to know if deal breakers are a good thing, or do we perhaps need to set them aside so that we don't miss out on someone who has potential?

I told him I think some deal breakers are important (e.g., you're very religious and want to have someone who shares your views) while others can be set aside (he needs to make $X, or be X height or have all his hair!).

I've heard of some common deal breakers:

- Height
- Weight
- Age
- Smoking
- Bad teeth

- Personal hygiene
- Bad dresser
- Too talkative
- Too self-absorbed
- Too shy
- Negative
- Mean
- Rude
- Excessive cursing
- Table manners
  (chews with mouth open, eats salad with fingers, bends head to plate to eat)
- Religion
- Politics
- Intelligence (too much or not enough)
- Education
- Finances
- Kids (you have them and he doesn't like kids, he has them and you don't like kids or feel he won't have any time for you, or one of you wants kids and the other doesn't)

My deal breakers mostly have to do with how someone treats me

I talked about a few more that are apparent on the first date in "Women's first-date blunders" and "First-date red flags that this guy isn't for you" (both in the *First-Rate First Dates: Increase the Chance of a Second Date* book).

Some of the ones I'm surprised by are the ones I think are sort of minor:

💜 A woman jettisons a man the first time he doesn't call when he says he will, without giving him a chance to explain, and even though he's called on time every other time.

💜 He wears Birkenstocks and she's a wingtip kind of gal.

💜 She puts lipstick on at the restaurant table.

💜 He won't buy her expensive jewelry even through they've only dated a month.

💜 He doesn't drive an expensive car.

The reporter asked if I had deal breakers in my own dating life. Yes. They mostly have to do with how someone treats me.

💜 If he is mean or inconsiderate, I won't tolerate that — at least after I give him some grace for the first time in case there was some unusual cause. I give people a lot of slack, but meanness is inexcusable.

💜 I'm not very tolerant of someone who takes me for granted.

💜 I have no patience for someone who doesn't act with integrity.

♥ Since I'm 5'10" I'm afraid I'm not keen on going out with someone who's shorter. I know this isn't an issue for many women (like Katie Holmes or Nicole Kidman), but it is for me.

What are your deal breakers? Any that you know are perhaps a bit frivolous, but are important to you?

How does music affect your dating?

Listening to my preferred radio station today, I noticed how many of my favorite songs are love ballads. Not lyrics of heartbreak and disappointment, but songs of deep caring and affection. Okay, I admit it, in addition to Luther Vandross, Marvin Gaye, Toni Braxton, Babyface, Gladys Knight and Michael Bolton, I like tunes by Barry White, which are not all exactly tender love songs. But they are sexy.

I noticed how my heart has ached to be loved by someone the same way the lyricist described — and to love someone similarly in return. The ardor described seems so deep and unshakable. Is it all an unattainable fantasy?

It got me thinking whether we choose our favorite music based on our feelings toward love and life, or if our feelings of love and live are shaped by the music we hear. They seem to go hand in hand.

If you are pessimistic about love, does downer music contribute to that feeling? Some teenagers are known to

have listened to head-banging heavy metal before com-
mitting suicide or harming others. If you listen to music
where the men are two-timers, players, cads and jerks,
or derogatory toward women, does that reflect how you
view men?

So if you start listening to love ballads, will that help
you have a more hopeful attitude toward finding a great
guy? And then you're more likely to find one? Or will it
depress you that you don't have one?

What kind of music do you listen to and how do you
think it affects your attitude about love? And if you find
you listen to pessimistic music and want to see if opti-
mistic music might help you change your attitude, will
you experiment with it and tell us what happened?

What melts your heart?

We all dream of someone who melts our heart. And when he does or says those liquefying actions or words, his flaws seem to dim. We are drawn to him more. We feel ourselves rising a bit more towards love.

What are not just things you like, but things that make your heart soften? Are there phrases you know make your knees weak when you hear them? Are there actions that are just so loving that you are then putty in his hands? I know certain actions make me swoon, and then there are others that I don't know get me giddy until I hear or experience them.

To help you get started on your list, here are some examples of what a man I dated for 3 months wrote in emails that left me in a puddle, even before we met:

- "I've appreciated your sexy way of approaching life. You've moved me in a high school crush kind of way."

- "You realize I'm falling in e-love with you. I know that's e-wrong, since we just e-met. I'll see an e-therapist to stay e-grounded."

"You, my exciting, intelligent, beautiful inside and out professional, are a wonderful muse. I have been energized by you and, at the risk of quoting another movie, 'You make me want to be a better man.'"

"I just want to make it clear that I am hoping for a very long-term relationship with you."

"I want you to feel warm, safe and cherished."

"I'd like to think I'm going to be able to love you for the rest of time."

"I am in total awe of you and my love for you is oozing out of me in bright thoughts, smiles, and even that stupid laugh I do."

"I'm up … woke up thinking of you and got too excited to sleep."

"You're a princess and I miss you very much."

"If I were with you I would give you such a long, loving kiss it would take your breath away."

"You know how special you are to me and you ARE a glorious, gorgeous, and generous Goddess. This man is so grateful to God to have found you."

"I may not be there in person, but I'm there in loving, honoring spirit."

"Only 5 days until I get to see you again."

- "I'm thinking about you"
- "I miss you."
- "I love you."

What gets your knees weak?

Are parts of you excellent?

shleigh Brilliant writes clever sayings that make you laugh or think. Part of his, well, brilliance is that the sayings are limited to a maximum of 17 words. He is one of the most widely-quoted living writers, and also the highest-paid (per word).

One of my favorite Pot Shots (which his musings are called) is the name of one of his books.

I May Not Be Totally Perfect, But Parts of Me Are Excellent

This is a good dating mantra. When you begin to focus on your imperfections (body shape, skin, wrinkles, hair, teeth, "baggage"), it is easy to forget that there are parts of you that are stupendous. Maybe it's your quick wit, infectious laugh, great listening, continual thoughtfulness or loving compassion.

The guy who is for you will love you for all of your parts, not just the excellent ones. It's the imperfect bits that make you the interesting and enticing creature you are.

And it also keeps you humble! Imagine how easy it would be to be arrogant if everything was flawless? My experience is the folks who are most arrogant have major imperfections and they use haughtiness to try to mask these failings.

Part of Cindy Crawford's allure is her mole. Angelina Jolie's overlarge lips are considered sexy. Mona Lisa's smile is enigmatic. Imagine how she'd look with a big smile flashing perfect, pure-white teeth.

Celebrate your unusualness. Perfection is boring and unattainable. Your atypical parts make you special, unique and rare. They are what makes you you. Which is, no doubt, excellent.

At www.AshleighBrilliant.com you'll see Ashleigh's various products, including postcards, books, t-shirts, mugs, pillows, and hats and his over 9000 Pot Shots.

What makes you feel sexy?

In "What is sexy?" (in the *From Fear to Frolic: Get Naked Without Getting Embarrassed* book) I asked you to explore what you think is sexy in a man. Now I'd like you to identify what makes you feel sexy.

For some women, it is when they feel fit and healthy. When they neglect their workout routine, they feel sluggish and not at the top of their game. They don't feel as confident or flirty.

Other women feel sexy when they wear fun, well-fitting clothing that flatters their figures. Some feel sexy in tight jeans, others in more relaxed slacks, and some when wearing swingy skirts. Others find power suits bring out the best in them, sometimes coupled with lacy lingerie.

Shoes are another tool. By changing footwear a woman can go from feeling matronly to red hot. A difference between a flat and a 2"- 3" heel can change an outfit — and attitude — dramatically. And for many, thinner heels feel sexier than thick, clunky ones. Some women find strappy sandals appealing, while others love how pumps make them feel. However, for a women who's uncomfortable in heels, flats are sexier because she's more at ease.

Makeup helps some women feel fetching. Applied in the quantity and style for one's comfort level, some feel it covers flaws and accentuates positive features. Others eschew estheticians' aids because to them it feels fake and unnatural.

Strut your mojo no matter where you are.

And for some of us, it's our hair. While clothes, makeup and a healthy body contribute to my feeling sexy, I've learned that one of the biggest pieces of the puzzle is my hair. Generally, I love my hair, as it's thick — 4 times normal I'm told. It's naturally wavy, but sometimes I flat iron it. Other times I curl it and it bounces. I like to wear it longer — a few inches below my shoulders. But I've instructed my stylist to hack it back when I begin to look like those middle-aged women who wear longer hair trying to look 30 again. That is unattractive.

Recently it slipped into the danger zone. She pruned 3 inches, which left me with an above-the-shoulder bob. It immediately affected my feeling of sexiness. Silly, I know, since I'm the same playful, flirty, fun, sensual woman who entered the salon with longer hair. But upon leaving, I felt more frumpish. I know that with the right makeup, clothes and shoes I'll feel sexy again. And of course, I can let it grow out again. But I find it astounding what a difference 3 inches can make.

Years ago, a different stylist cut my hair short, a few inches long. I looked like a brunette, female version of Rod Stewart, but not as thin. I cried myself to sleep. I had repeatedly told her that I needed to have some curl to my hair to feel feminine. She ignored me one too many times. That was the last time she had me as a customer.

I look at beauties like Halle Berry or Jada Pinkett Smith and notice the length of their hair — or a shaved head — doesn't affect their sexiness. They express their mojo no matter what they are wearing or how they are coiffed. Of course, they have stunningly beautiful faces, so their hair is superfluous.

So what makes you feel sexy? If you can articulate it, you're more likely to make sure you feel sexy — and show it — when out on a date, or even just around town. You never know who you'll run into at the produce section of your grocery store. Strut your mojo no matter where you are.

Make sure to download your free
eBook Attract Your Next Great Mate:
Dating Advice From Top Relationship Experts *at www.DatingGoddess.
com/freebie*

Are you arguing your limitations?

 idlife women sometimes passionately, convincingly, compellingly tell me why no man would be interested in dating them. "Men aren't interested in a woman like me who has wrinkles, bags, extra pounds and hot flashes," she may start. "They're only interested in girls half their age. And forget anyone wanting a feisty, intelligent, educated woman like me. They are too threatened by us," she continues. And if I let her, she'll go on. And on. And on.

In "There must be a pony in here," (see page 143) I quoted Richard Bach's book *Illusions: The Adventures of a Reluctant Messiah*. One of my favorite quotes from the book is:

"Argue your limitations and they are yours."

The more you argue why no one would be interested in you, the more you convince yourself. Then you close yourself off from anyone who is the slightest bit interested. The 50-ish man who talked to you at length at the party the other night? He was very nice, funny, intelligent, and even kinda cute, but he wouldn't be interested in someone like you. No, you're sure of that. In fact, you saw him later talking to a 30-something beauty. But he left alone, you noticed.

What about that friend of your co-worker's who you met at her birthday bash? He was really fun and you enjoyed bantering with him. But he was a successful executive and ran marathons, so he would probably have disdain for your out-of-shape body.

The interesting owner of your favorite restaurant? You frequent it regularly, and he's always nice, even flirty. But you're sure he's just doing that because you're his customer. He probably has a girlfriend, but you know he's not married because he's not wearing a wedding ring. Besides, he'd probably rather be with a foodie — someone who understands his business.

Do you ever hear yourself having similar conversations in your mind? You are arguing your limitations. You are stopping any possibility of getting to know these guys better and perhaps going out, even if just for coffee. And if you suggest coffee and he says he's in a relationship, so what? You've made his day by showing he's attractive, and even if the relationship isn't revealed until during coffee, you may have a new great pal.

So if you hear yourself arguing for your limitations, tell yourself to stop it immediately. Remind yourself you would be an interesting companion for a number of men. And open yourself up to the possibilities.

Are you too picky?

A friend chided me, "You've gone out with 75 men in 2 years. Why aren't you married? Are you too picky?"

When midlife women share that they haven't found their "one" and they're getting tired of looking, they begin to wonder if they are being too picky. The dilemma is, should you continue to be picky, perhaps taking a long time to meet someone who meets your important criteria, or should you accept someone who meets most, but not all, of your "must haves"?

A friend who's been married 25 years shared that while she loves her husband very much, there are things she would prefer were different about him. She says, "Did I settle? In some ways, yes. However, he has many qualities I adore. But he's also missing some things that would make us more compatible."

I wonder how much of this is our needs changing over time. What she wanted/needed 25 years ago is different now that they are empty-nesters and looking to entertain themselves pre-retirement. While we're not in a relationship, we can determine what we want now, but we also need to project what we think we want for the next 10, 20, 30 or more years.

Many dating advisers recommend you come up with no more than 5 "must have" characteristics about your ideal guy. Other preferences beyond that are negotiable. I've heard about women having 20-100 "must have" deal breakers. I think that's over the top. However, many midlife women feel, "I have a full, rich, great life. I don't need a man. So for me to give up time with my friends, work, or hobbies, he needs to be spectacular. And here's my list of what spectacular is."

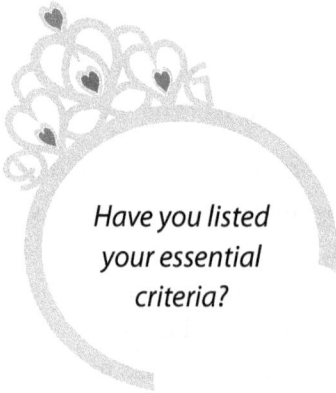

Have you listed your essential criteria?

Have you listed your essential criteria? Most daters have. "Someone nice" is a common response. "Someone loving." You need to be more specific than that.

Equally important to what you want is what would make you feel you settled? And if a guy has much of what's on your "must have" list but not all, are you willing to give him a chance to see if you can live with that and love him without feeling that you settled? And if he knows he doesn't measure up in one area and is willing to work on it, will you give him some time to do so?

Turn your liabilities
into assets

Years ago I led a seminar on how to have a positive attitude at work. In the text, *Attitude: Your Most Priceless Possession,* author Elwood Chapman suggests employing the "Flipside Technique."

The concept is to take something not commonly considered good and reframe it as a positive, injecting a dose of humor when necessary. We'll explore how to practice this in midlife dating, as most women have trouble moving past what they see as their flaws. (See "Are you describing yourself compellingly?" in the *Winning at the Online Dating Game: Stack the Deck in Your Favor* book.)

Let give you some non-dating examples first.

❤ In "I'm glad dating is hard" (see the *Date or Wait: Are You Ready for Mr. Great?* book) I shared how the late motivational speaker Art Berg was grateful he broke his neck as it made him reach deep for inner resources he might not have otherwise tapped. He used humor in his talks to illustrate how he learned to stretch beyond what he thought was possible.

💜 Vintage VW Beetle commercials promoted how small is beautiful, how economical Beetles were, and how the diminutive car was perfect for those who didn't march in lockstep with everyone else. One ad's caption said, "It makes your house look bigger." Another, "Live below your means." It took what would be considered drawbacks — smallness, low price and ugliness — and turned them into assets.

💜 Southwest Airlines turned no frills — including no meals nor reserved seats — into a competitive advantage. Their ads and staff approach their limitations with humor and fun. It allows them to keep their prices low, which they tout in their marketing.

💜 A client of mine, the facilities department for a large company, is working on fun ways to counter complaints they can do little about. They can't make everyone happy about office temperature. So we're playing with designing posters that suggest the top 10 things to do if you're too hot in your office, such as wearing your bathing suit at work, soaking your feet in a tub of ice and using the company phone directory as a fan.

How can you apply this to midlife dating? Take what you think of as a liability and turn it into asset

♥ Overweight — More of me to love. I'll enjoy dining with you, not pick at my food.

♥ Wrinkles — I enjoy life and laugh a lot.

♥ Kids — A ready-made excuse to go to the zoo, amusement parks, county fairs, and animated films.

♥ Limited time to date — You'll get my focus when we're together, and the anticipation of seeing each other will make our time even sweeter.

♥ Health or physical challenges — We can slow the pace so we can savor life rather than dashing hither and yon.

What do you consider a liability and how could you Flipside it?

Are you ready to pick a guy?

A former beau and I had an email conversation today. He saw my profile again listed on a few dating sites and asked what was happening. I explained about the recent meltdown of a relationship and he suggested we should get back together.

I tried to reply pleasantly but still let him know I'm not interested in him romantically. I said, "You have a lot to offer the right woman." (When I shared this response with a male friend, he made a gagging expression. So how do you tell someone gently — and repeatedly — that you're not attracted to him? He's a good guy, not a toad. I've written about him before in "He wants romance; you want friendship," in the *Move On Gracefully: Break Up Without Heartache* book.)

We mused about dating life. I've been dating 3.5 years, he's been at it four. He, like me, has had lots of first dates, and a few multi-month relationships. He's 61 and getting tired of the hunt. He said:

"I know this is crazy but at this point in our lives,

with the amount of time we have left, we either choose to stay single or better yet, contrive a great relationship and tolerate the best possible person we can find and don't argue with them. I'm not saying be passive, but tolerant and forgiving of the other's attitudes and preferences. Then all you have left is great fun, great sex, great traveling, and love."

While I understand his point, I'm not quite ready to just choose someone and decide he's The One. However I have been interested in what happens in arranged marriages. I asked those whose marriages were arranged how they felt about marrying someone with whom they weren't in love. The overwhelming response is,"You learn to love them." As long as there isn't abuse of any kind, and their mate is a decent, caring, sane person, they have found ways to learn to love him/her.

> I'm not quite ready to just choose someone and decide he's The One.

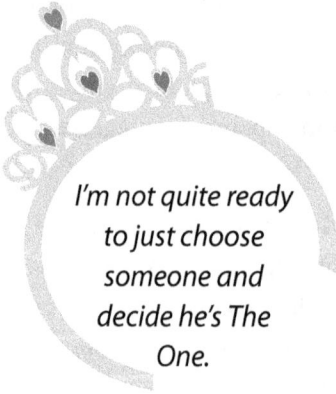

In an arranged marriage others make the decision; the families do the due diligence for you. In our world, we make the decision, sometimes not doing any due diligence. If someone has many of the characteristics you want, and a few that drive you crazy, can you still learn to love him? Are we too quick to throw the baby out with the bath water if we find someone with whom we're generally compatible?

Or would that be settling? If you felt you settled, would you ever be happy? Or is the elusive soul mate just a myth? Real-life couples who seem to have fabulous relationships don't share their setbacks, so it appears they are madly in love for years and years. And maybe they are.

What do you think? After dating a while and finding some "almost-perfect" guys, should you just choose to be with the next one who seems pretty darn good, even with some glaring warts? Or should you hold out for one for whom you can fall head over heels and he for you? Is there a point where you need to decide to wait no longer?

Are you a dating "hypertaster"?

You are thinking, "What is DG talking about? What the heck is a hypertaster? And what can it possibly do with dating?"

Let me explain. Yesterday, I had a fabulous day at Copia, the American center for wine, food and the arts in Napa, CA. Being a self-admitted wine dolt, I spent the day taking classes and touring the exhibits and gardens. I started with "Winetasting 101 and progressed through "Winetasting 102," "Zinfandel Madness," and ending with "Introduction to Wine & Food Pairing." Each program was led by an amazingly interesting and knowledgeable wine educator.

I have always felt I had an unsophisticated palate because I don't like most wine. I would be embarrassed when clients or colleagues would rave about the Cabernet or Merlot being served, and I could barely endure a sip. I thought my Kansas-born taste buds were undeveloped as I stuck to less trendy Rieslings and Gewurztraminers.

In the last class, I learned that I am one of the 25%

of the population considered a "hypertaster" or "super-taster." This means we taste tannin, spices, bitterness, and other flavors much more intensely than the other 75% of the population. This explains why I don't enjoy most wines, as many have tannin as a key component.

According to Linda Bartoshuk, Ph.D., a professor of surgery at the Yale University School of Medicine, hypertasters are genetically engineered to have over 38-100 times as many taste buds as a "non-taster," which is 25% of the population.

I began to think of this in terms of dating. In "Are you ready to pick a guy?" (page 59) and "Are you too picky?" (page 53) we discussed how some daters seem not to be able to find someone for a LTR who is to their taste. I'm curious if this inability to find a delicious match has anything to do with one's physical tasting ability. I wonder if we hypertasters are genetically predisposed to be pickier? Most of the population — an estimated 50% — are considered "regular tasters." One article on tasting hypersensitivity quotes Dr. Bartoshuk, "'The world is built for regular tasters,' noting that such people experience foods as not too sweet, bitter, salty or sour." I wonder if that holds for their taste in a mate, too? They are more tolerant, less picky, easier to please.

What do you notice about your own tastes in food and taste in men? Do you think you're a non-taster, regular taster, or supertaster?

How does your parents' relationship affect yours?

Our parents are often our role models for relationships, for better or worse. No matter how much I rejected my parents' toxic relationship as a template, I'm sure messages of how a couple treats one another were deeply embedded in my psyche.

When my mother was a young woman, she had multiple prospective suitors. She and her girlfriends volunteered to entertain the troops by attending USO dances for soldiers stationed at the nearby military base. She was a fetching, slender, curvy, well-dressed beauty, so she caught the eye of many. My father wooed her in person then through letters from his front-line encampment in the Philippines.

Many men had been interested in courting her. Knowing this, and knowing that my parents' relationship was tumultuous even from the beginning — including fighting on their wedding day—— near the end of her life I asked why she agreed to marry him.

"Because he looked so handsome in his uniform," she replied.

"Didn't other soldiers look handsome in their uniforms? Other men who weren't so quarrelsome? Who treated you better?"

She said he looked the best to her, even more so than officers who were sweet on her.

Was this the primary husband-choosing criterion for a 21-year-old, naive, Kansas farm girl? She was smart — she skipped second grade — so why would she not think how her life would be with this contentious man who got fired or quit all jobs within 2 weeks in

How much of your parents' mate selection decisions are you prone to repeat?

their first 4 years of marriage? Did she not think beyond his uniformed looks for other signs of future happiness?

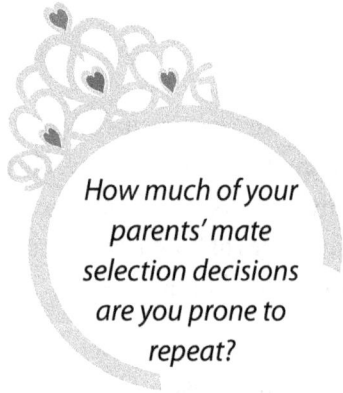

How much of your parents' mate selection decisions are you prone to repeat? Are you conscious of why your parents chose each other, and how that may impact how you choose potential mates?

My mother quickly regretted marrying the man who

looked so handsome in his uniform. He seemed to always be threatened by her superior intelligence, and his low self-esteem surfaced in his frequent bickering with her and others, resulting in lost jobs, wrecked friendships, and strained family relationships. But after we kids came along, she felt trapped, as a divorce attorney she visited painted an even more dismal picture of her life if she left him. She never did get the confidence to leave the toxic relationship.

How have your parents' relationship dynamics affected your romances? Even if you consciously reject what you don't like about their interactions, might there be some subliminal messages that surface when you're dating?

The fear of finding "The One"

Wwe can call it commitment phobia. But before we label it, let's examine it. I'd bet it has happened to nearly all of us at one time or another.

You meet someone terrific, and he feels similarly. You date for a while — months or even years. You say you are committed to each other, maybe even engaged, but the relationship does not progress beyond sharing each other's lives — and beds — several times a week.

Many people say this shows a commitment problem or immaturity on one or both people's part. However, for the couple it may be just fine to have your own space and not want to be together full time. If you live within a reasonable driving distance, it may work well for both.

The complication comes when one or both of you would have to make a big change to be together frequently. If you live far enough apart, multiple visits each week can become a hassle, no matter how wonderful your time together is. If your homes are too small to easily accommodate another person, or if the commute to each other's place is onerous, something will need to change to keep the relationship together. One or both of you will need to move.

Some people try to stave off having to make decisions like this by purposefully avoiding dating people who are outside a reasonable commute difference. Unfortunately, their heart hasn't heard of this love perimeter, so they may fall for someone regardless of their boundary.

I had a conversation with an astute, conscious, self-aware, long-single friend who shared that the dramatic changes involved when one has found The One have kept him from pursuing serious relationships. While one could diss him as immature, selfish, or commitment phobic, I applaud his insight.

Do you have any fears that go hand in hand with finding The One?

I've examined this for myself, noting that I've not been in any serious relationships during my 3.5 years of dating, while other divorcées are often remarried in this time frame. If you have been dating for a while, is there a lingering concern that a major lifestyle change will have to happen when you meet The One? You'd have to modify things in your life that are working for you, whether it's your ability to do whatever you want when you want or having to clean out closet space and drawers if he were to move into your place. Or you'd have to shoehorn your belongings into his place, or you'd move to a new place together. While some people find change exciting, others find major change wrought with concerns, like what if it doesn't work out after you've made these big changes.

Do you have any fears that go hand in hand with finding The One? If so, share them so others can learn from you.

Are you set in your ways?

A complaint I hear from midlife daters is that others they date seem set in their ways. This can become evident on the first date or it may take a while. But for those who this describes, it eventually comes out.

It might be an unwillingness to try a new cuisine, refusal to travel abroad, or opposition to watching a different movie genre. It could be habits that won't budge: not allowing anyone else to sit in his TV-room chair, rejecting invitations to go out on favorite TV nights, or not wanting to try any new activities.

Some midlife daters seem to want to date only on their own terms: with a specific type of person, on only certain nights per week, for only so many hours, doing activities with which he is already comfortable. The concept of dating really means having a companion when he wants her to accompany him on what he wants to do and when he wants to do it. (Although I am using the male pronoun, we all know women who fit this description.)

It's easy to point a finger at others and spotlight their failings. It's harder to turn around that finger and ask yourself the pointed question: Are you set in your ways?

💜 How open are you to new activities? Do you like to try new things, or do you do them begrudgingly?

💜 Do you expect a man to join you in your activities but decline his invitations to join him in his favorite pastimes that may not (yet) be at the top of your list?

Some midlife daters seem to want to date only on their own terms

💜 Are you comfortable mixing things up sometimes just to get a new perspective? Moving the furniture, trying new restaurants, visiting new places?

💜 If someone upsets your way of doing things, are you tolerant and at peace? If he sits in your place at the table, wants you to join him in a dance class on your TV night, or takes you to an unusual restaurant, do you jump in feet first — or with feet dragging?

If you find yourself stuck in routines, try forcing yourself to mix it up. Instead of staying in on TV night, set up Tivo or DVR and accept your neighbor's long-standing invitation to join her at her line-dancing lessons. If you always go to the movies with your gal pals on Friday nights, see if they'll agree to karaoke instead. Move the living room furniture. Sleep on the other side of the bed. Change "your" spot at the kitchen table. Drive a new way to work. Go to that new ethnic restaurant you've been meaning to try.

Experiment with new things. You won't like them all. But by expanding your choices you open yourself up to new possibilities and will find some new favorites. And you'll be more appealing to a broader range of men.

Have you done inner work?

Adventures in Delicious Dating After 40 reader Tim asked me to address the following, which applies to both genders:

> I'm 41 and been dating 3 years. Most of the woman I meet assume that they can go from a divorce to another long-term relationship and never work on themselves before doing so. The longer someone is in a bad relationship the more work it is going to take to get yourself ready to date and have a healthy relationship again.

> I spent 5 years in a 12-step program designed for family members of substance abusers, and even longer in personal counseling. I slowly changed myself into an emotionally healthy person capable of a healthy relationship.

> I realize most people are not going to have gone through the level of self-improvement as I have. I do not believe I have unattainable criteria by which I'm judging my dates, and which have been

confirmed by other emotionally healthy people. But I wonder if I'm ever going to find someone who admits that both partners in a failed marriage are responsible to some degree. If you've been in an abusive situation, you're going to need to seek help if you plan on having a healthy relationship again.

Here are responses from women when I asked what they had done since their divorce to ensure a better outcome in their next relationship.

"I've been divorced for a year, and my ex was such an a–hole I knew I needed to take care of myself a little so just went shopping." The sad part is she meant it.

"It was entirely his fault, why should I have to do anything?" Next please!

A woman I dated for several months gave me all of the right answers. Turns out she knew the right things to say, but saying them and living them are two completely different things. She had major trust issues with men in general because of how terribly her ex had treated her. This caused communication problems because she was still trying to protect herself from him, even though she was dating me.

How can women (or men) expect to move onto an emotionally healthy relationship when they have only ever been in a bad one without doing anything to change?

Tim, you articulate what I and other midlife daters have found as well. Few are willing to look at their part in a marriage breakdown as it is so much easier to blame the one who "did you wrong." Since my ex left me (not for another woman), it was easy to blame him for being self-centered and inflexible. But the more I looked inside, I saw I had a hand in our dissolution, even though it was hard to admit it.

I find few people willing to look inside, even if they are in a terrific relationship. It takes courage to face your demons. Although it's gotten much better in the last few decades, there is still some stigma about counseling. Many people feel they aren't "broken" so why invest in counseling? The truth is a good counselor can help you become even better than you imagined, clearing out old issues that may be holding you back without your realizing it. In the past 30 years I've seen therapists when I've been in pain and also when I wanted to make my life even better. But it can be emotionally draining, so I can see why many people prefer not to experience reliving painful pasts.

Few are willing to look at their part in a marriage breakdown

Now, back to the women's responses to your question. While shopping therapy can be beneficial, it is not if that's the only thing you've done to heal from the relationship.

And even if your ex was the biggest cad, jerk, loser and player ever born, there is still healing to do about what caused you to be attracted to someone like this or stay with someone like that. If you don't work on the root causes, you'll keep finding yourself with the same kind of person, no matter how much you swear you know the signs.

To answer your specific question, I'm biased. I think you are doomed to repeat the same type of relationship issues with the next relationship(s) until you do some reflection, introspection and work on recognizing the causes of your patterns. If someone I'm dating admits he's never done any personal growth activities, I'm cautious. However, I know the opposite is also a red flag — if someone is constantly enrolled in self-development programs, but makes no changes. They just know the language but don't practice the principles.

What do you think? Do you think it's important to work on yourself before entering your next relationship? What has worked for you? How do you respond to a potential suitor who says he doesn't need to do any reflection and takes no part of the responsibility for his last relationship failing?

Consciously creating the relationship you want

"Don't let what you've created get in the way of what you want to create." —Jana Stanfield

My friend Jana Stanfield, the amazing musical artist, said this as we talked about our somewhat recent singlehood and what we could do with our lives now that we didn't have a husband about whom to be concerned. We were sharing our travel lust and how responsibilities at home can keep you feeling that you can't do what you've always wanted to do, like extended travel. The world we'd created — including a home with a mortgage and other responsibilities — could get in the way of the life for which we've longed.

What does this have to do with dating? I think it relates because sometimes once we get a sweetie — something we've created — we don't really know if this relationship is what we want. Yes, we've been in other — maybe a number — of long-term relationships. But the person you are right now hasn't. Hopefully you've learned more about what makes relationships work as well as dissolve, and about yourself as you've moved through life's journey. So you are a more savvy person entering a new relationship.

But since we've longed for someone in our life, we cling to the connection, even though once we're into it, we may realize it isn't what we really want. How much of this is fear, fickleness, and immaturity? Who's to say? For discussion, let's say these aren't factors. We are present to the time and effort it took to find the guy and develop a bond to become sweeties. We've worked through some hiccups and are fond of him. But we realize that being with him will preclude us from having the life we want to create.

We cling to the connection

You owe it to both of you to discuss the disconnect. Maybe his career has required him to live in his industry's hub and you've assumed that means he'll never move. Or perhaps you've thought his nearby family would keep him anchored in this spot. You have dreams of living somewhere else. Once your goals are shared, you may learn that he's been yearning for a change and he'd be delighted to step toward the life you want to create.

But maybe you will discover that you both have very different pictures of the future. So although you wanted to create a loving relationship with someone like him, you have to decide which dream is more important. If you have to choose, you must be very clear which is more critical to your happiness because if you make the decision to subjugate your other goals to stay with him, you very likely will resent him. And if you abandon him to move toward the life you want to create, you may become lonely and sad to leave him behind.

Have you created something in your life that is getting in the way of your creating the life you want? If so, write it down and what you can do about it.

Do you know what will make you happy?

When dating someone with whom you've become enamored, it is easy to project your life into the future. You imagine being intertwined every blissful day, moving in together, perhaps getting married. In this fantasy is embedded perpetual elation, constant joy, unbridled happiness.

Wouldn't it be grand if we could accurately predict such euphoria? Unfortunately, humans are unskilled at foretelling what really will make them happy.

Ironically, on our first date a gentleman gave me a copy of *Stumbling on Happiness* by Daniel Gilbert. It was ironic because I then applied the author's concepts to dating. And when I imagined a possible future relationship with this man, I couldn't conjure up an image of us together! We parted ways after the second date.

In the Amazon.com editorial review of the book, Daphne Durham writes,

> *"Do you know what makes you happy? Daniel*

Gilbert would bet that you think you do, but you are most likely wrong."

Gilbert shares example of studies that show how humans are pretty inept at predicting what will make us happy in the future. So you think a great, loving, charming guy will make you happy until the end of time? Maybe. Maybe not. Malcolm Gladwell adds in his review of the book, "We're terrible at knowing how we will feel a day or a month or year from now, and even worse at know-ing what will and will not bring us that cherished happiness.... Our imaginations are really bad at tell-ing us how we will think when the fu-ture finally comes. And our personal experiences aren't nearly as good at correcting these errors as we might think."

You imagine being intertwined every blissful day

If we believe Gilbert's concepts, based largely on psychological research, then what are we to do? Give up reaching for what we think will make us happy? Only live in the present without striving for any betterment in our condition, which we think will make us happier?

In "Are you a happy dater?" (page 151) I discuss how my friend the late Art Berg, a paraplegic, decided to be happy every day. He didn't focus on the past and what he'd lost before his accident, nor the future and how his life may be cut short because of his condition. By not predicting what would make him happy in the future, he avoided disappointment.

I think it takes a special mindset to accomplish not wanting to project what will make us happy. We take what we've learned from past relationships and couple that with who we know ourself to be now, and say, "I want a man who… and with whom I can have a relationship like…." We feel our past will inform our decisions that will create our future.

But then a man waltzes in who matches very few of our "must have" criteria and sweeps us off our feet. So much for our predictions and "perfect man" list!

The strong vs. nice woman debate

*Why Men Love Bitches: From Doormat to Dreamgirl —
A Woman's Guide to Holding Her Own in a Relationship*
by Sherry Argov

First, let me allow the author to explain the title, as it is somewhat off-putting to those of us who don't relish being referred to as bitches. Argov writes "I'm not recommending that a woman have an abrasive disposition. The woman I'm describing is kind yet strong. She doesn't give up her life, and she won't chase a man." Of course, *Why Men Love Confident Women* wouldn't have garnered the same kind of press, so she went with a more sensational title.

I agree with some of what she says. I saw myself both as a strong woman standing up for myself as well as a "nice" woman who has allowed myself in the past to get taken for granted.

Other advice was the opposite of my values. For example, she advocates being "dumb like a fox." I read this chapter as how to play games. You don't tell the man directly what you want or are upset about, you show it by your actions. For example, the man you're dating calls you at 10 p.m. to say he misses you and wants you to come over and cuddle. You are irritated that he wants you to drive to his place for a booty call. But do you say that? No. That would be too direct. Instead, you tell him you're slipping into something sexy and will be over in 5 minutes. Could he wait you outside with an umbrella since it's raining? (I don't know why he wouldn't suggest you bring your own umbrella, but hey, this is Argov's book.) He waits, and waits, and waits and you don't arrive. After an hour, it dawns on him you're not coming and he was being a lout!

Or to show your live-in beau he can't control you, you stay out 2 hours after you told him you'd be home, without calling. That is downright rude to me, and I'd be worried sick if someone I cared about was two hours late and didn't let me know they were okay.

Her point is that men don't hear words, they only see actions. They won't hear that you're upset with them. They tune it out as if you're nagging. Isn't this a tad condescending? It implies all men are uncommunicative and unable to talk about issues openly, honestly and maturely.

The book was confusing because she says bitches are nice, but nice gals get treated like doormats. But the examples she gave showing when strong women were nice revealed they were duplicitous and passive aggressive, not saying what they were feeling or wanted.

I like the general message that you need to be clear

on what you want and not change who you are to fit what you think your guy wants. This means don't give up your gym time, gal pals and other self-care priorities. She says you need to look out for yourself all the time, and the more you do the more appealing you will be to men. The more you acquiesce and change your life to constantly accommodate his preferences, he loses respect for you. Which means he'll go poof in an instant.

> *You need to look out for yourself all the time*

In "Do men want feisty women?" (see *Embracing Midlife Men: Insights Into Curious Behaviors* book) we discussed that many men like spirited, strong women. When I bounced off the book's premise to a guy pal I adore, he said, "I don't think most guys are attracted to strong women. I think they scare the pants off the guys." I can see it would with some men, but I also know some won't put up with a dependent woman. The key is to figure out who you are and what you want, then find a way to attract what is a good fit for you.

What's your opinion about the book's teachings? Do you think it is best to not say what you want but show through your actions/inactions?

Conflicting dating advice

D o you experience conflicting Dating Advice From relationship "experts" and/or savvy friends? I do. While I share my insights, lessons and yes, sometimes advice on this blog, there are many issues about dating I'm still figuring out.

A current dilemma is around whether to cook for a potential suitor I had several dates with many months ago. Some time ago he did me a giant favor, and I offered to cook him dinner to show my gratitude. He declined at the time saying I didn't have to do that. Now, many months later, with no communication in between, he emails "You still owe me dinner." While I'd love to see him, I'm not feeling as beholden as I did when the offer was tendered, and I'm a little miffed that he hasn't communicated a peep in the interim months. I'm not really feeling I want to knock myself out cooking for him, but I would like to see him.

If you believe *Why Men Love Bitches*, you would cook nearly never for a guy you're dating, as you don't want to be seen in a mother role. Contrast that with the counsel of a wise friend who's taken courses on understanding men. She reiterates the old adage about the best way to a man's heart being through his stomach and that cooking is just the thing to endear a guy to you. As long, of course, that you wear something appealing if not sexy, and not your mother's apron and baggy dress.

And others on the "cook for him" side of the ledger would say if he's taken you out to dinner several times, you reciprocate by cooking for him. But the "don't cook" argument would be led by the "don't try to even the score" aficionados. A friend says offer a picnic with deli sandwiches or a take out meal, but I know he grows weary of store-bought food.

Another quandary I face is a man I haven't seen in a year nor talked to in seven months wants to see me again. When he went poof he had a very busy travel schedule and was only home 2 days/month for the several months we were in contact after we had three very good dates.

He's Just Not That Into You argues that if a guy is into you, he'll find 5 minutes to call and say "hi" several times a week, even when he's on the road. This guy didn't, so I assumed he must not be into me enough to call. He told me that he often worked 16-hour days on the road and didn't call his mother or grown kids either, so if I wanted to talk to him, just call. This didn't feel right to me, so after calling him a few times I stopped.

However, my aforementioned friend says that men compartmentalize, focus, and don't multitask as well as women. So it could very likely be true that this guy didn't think of anything else but work when he was away. And when he was home the few days a month, he had other issues to attend to.

Sounds like the excuses women make for men in *He's Just Not That Into You.*

Which advice do you listen to?

So which advice do you listen to? Ideally, you listen to the various input, then try to separate your rationalizations from your gut feelings. However, even your gut can be swayed by your heart, which can be coerced because of longing or loneliness to interpret signs the way you want to see them.

And where is the line between trying to truly understand and respond to how men think and playing games to manipulate them to do what you want? Where's the division between being honest and direct with your needs and desires vs. not sending him running with your straightforwardness?

I wish I had advice for you on this issue. This is one time I have more questions than answers. How do you sort out conflicting advice?

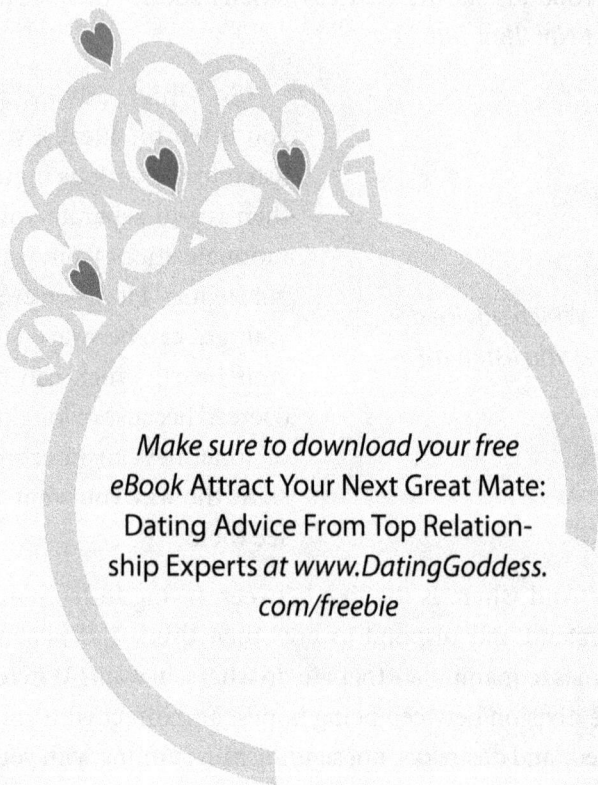

*Make sure to download your free
eBook* Attract Your Next Great Mate:
Dating Advice From Top Relationship Experts *at www.DatingGoddess.
com/freebie*

Dating data a dose of reality

Laws of the Jungle: Dating for Women Over 40 by Gloria MacDonald and Thelma Beam

I found this to be one of the most interesting books on midlife dating I've read in a long while. It is co-written by a matchmaker specializing in people over 40 (Gloria MacDonald), and a couples therapist (Thelma Beam). They blend data with examples from their practices to make an interesting book with many points I'd not read before. The book is not filled with silly games or "rules;" instead it is filled with facts based on the population of Canada and the US, as well as science. "What could be so interesting about facts in a dating book?" you ask.

Good question. The facts help the reader have a more grounded idea of what to expect in midlife dating, rather than a fantasy. And since many of us haven't dated for decades, it helps shower us in the icy water of reality.

"How could that possibly be helpful?" you may wonder. "Icy water is cold and bracing." You'd be right. But without the sobering facts, many women have pie-in-the-sky expectations. For example, the authors look at the data of how many single men and women there are in the US and Canada, minus a "kook" factor. They figured at age 45 there were 12 single women for every 10 single men. At age 55, there are 15 single women for every 10 men in this age group, and by 65 there are 10 men for 25 women. Of course, not every single person is looking for love, and some single people are in a committed relationship. But the numbers are awakening.

Midlife women often say, "I'm not making the first move," or "He has to work hard to win me," or "I'm not returning his call. I don't call men." While this mind set may have worked when they were in their 20's when there were more men than women, and the woman was in her prime, now in her 40's, 50's or 60's few men will work as hard as they did then. They just don't have to, as there are more women to choose from. Not that a woman should be easy, but she shouldn't insist he jump through so many hoops he'll be pooped.

Did you know that only 14% of men are 6-feet tall?

Midlife women also seem to be picky, their requirements often based on their ex or departed husband, without really a sense that they aren't in their 20's anymore. The majority of women say they want someone over 6-feet tall. Did you know that only 14% of men are

6-feet tall? Only 9% are 6'1'? Women of all heights say they want — in fact many say they require — a man who is at least 6-feet tall, even if she is under 5'10".

And many midlife women also insist that a man have all his hair. But 45% of men aged 40-49 have some hair loss; 55% of men 50-49; and 65% of men 60-69. Asking for all his hair is like a man insisting that a women has no gray in her hair, or doesn't dye her hair. It cuts down the options dramatically.

We know that both genders commonly list "slim, slender, fit" as their preferences for a partner. However, the data shows that 75% of people aged 45-74 are overweight. So if you insist on this, you're eliminating three-quarters of the population.

And lastly, women often say they want a successful man, stating they want someone who makes over $100,000/year — even if their ex or late husband didn't, or if she makes one-third of that. In the 45-64 age group, only 9-10% of men make six figures.

You may be saying, "But men are picky, too!" And you'd be right again. However, the data and our experience show that men date and marry women 5-30 years younger, so they have a much bigger pool to choose from. Of course, women are dating younger as well, but it is still most common for a woman to date someone nearer her own age or older. Which means the more insistent you are on certain external characteristics, the smaller the pool to choose from.

Does this mean you should settle? No, it means you

should be clear on the character of the man you want and how he will treat you and less hung up on characteristics, like hair, that are bound to change in a few years.

The book covers some "how to's" as well as the data, but that is not as interesting (at least to me). I will review the section on sex in another posting as I found their findings useful.

"I don't want to be hurt"

A man I met online shared this in an early email. His ex-wife cheated on him and he hasn't dated since his divorce seven years ago. He said it was because he didn't want to get hurt again.

I explained that nearly all relationships include some hurt at some point. Maybe it happens because of a misunderstanding or unmet expectations. But in all but rare cases there is some kind of hurt, especially in long-term relationships. Heck, hurt can occur with friends, but is more common with romantic situations as the expectations are higher.

Life — if you live it vigorously — involves risking hurt. When you put yourself out there, from asking for a date, to asking for a plum assignment at

Early all relationships include some hurt at some point.

work, you put yourself on the line. The stakes are higher the more emotionally involved you are. But if you don't take the risk to open your heart you'll also never have the possibility of deep love and connection.

When I think of risk and dating, I think of athletes. They risk injury every time they train for and play their sport. If they were afraid of injuring themselves, they would never practice nor play. How rewarding would that be?

So it is with romance. If you aren't willing to risk getting your heart bruised, you can never find love. And if you're very lucky, you'll never experience the pain of heartache. But if you do, know it is part of living and loving with gusto.

Is your sense of humor stunting your dating?

In many online profiles, both genders say they want a mate who possess a good sense of humor. But what really does that mean? For many, it means the man makes a funny (or almost funny) comment and the woman laughs.

But what if the woman is the funny (or funnier) one?

If you are the life of the party, some men are threatened. The person who gets others to laugh is the center of attention. This is a powerful position, as you hold court. "Making" someone laugh implies they can't help themselves — they must laugh. This shows you have wit, confidence, presence, popularity — and power.

In Gina Barreca's book, *They Used to Call Me Snow White…but I Drifted: Women's Strategic Use of Humor*, she mentions the findings of anthropologist Matadev Apte*. Gina says, "In communities around the world women who tell jokes are regarded as sexually promiscuous. The connection between humor and sexual invitation is made up of many links, among them the thought that it takes certain 'fallen' knowledge to make a joke."

I could understand if the jokes or wise cracks were bawdy, risqué, racy, suggestive, naughty, off-color, earthy, vulgar, crude, coarse, lewd, dirty, filthy, smutty, unseemly, X-rated, blue, or raunchy. But Dr. Apte doesn't distinguish what kind of jokes put you in the promiscuous category, just any woman who tells jokes. I'd guess those who make funny, witty remarks would also be categorized as loose women.

So that leaves women like Gina and me, and perhaps you, in an uncomfortable place. If we are witty and funny, as Gina definitely is and I can be, we are thought to be sluttish. But since making others laugh is also powerful, we are now powerful wanton women. Not something I have a lot of trouble with, and I doubt Gina does either. But it is interesting that for a woman, being funny can be a detriment in some situations.

If you are the life of the party, some men are threatened

I wonder if hilarious women like Lucille Ball, Phyllis Diller, Whoopie Goldberg, Paula Poundstone, and Gilda Radner ever felt their humor held them back when dating. Or did they just keep dating until they found a partner who appreciated their wise cracks?

That's my strategy. I'm proud that I was voted "Wittiest" by my high school classmates. I've had a room full of 1500 mostly male CEOs laughing. I used to crack up my ex. I'm not willing to dial it back because some man's ego can't take my being the center of attention for my witticisms. Nope. If he doesn't crack up too, we're not a good match.

What about you and your ability to make your date laugh? Do you find this is a good thing, or does it get in the way?

* *Humor and Laughter: An Anthropological Approach* by Matadev Apte

Relationship résumé

It's been said ad nauseam that dating is like job hunting. The online profile is the application, the first emails and call the screening process, the first date the initial interview, the second and subsequent dates are additional interviews. Following this metaphor, I guess you only get "offered the job" when you decide to be exclusive with your partner.

There are flaws in this parallel, of course, but a glaring one is the application process. Not only isn't all the information you want provided in an online profile, it is sometimes incorrect, just like in some résumés. However, we have to serve as our own fact checker.

What if we were to create our own relationship résumé to post on a web site or to send or hand to potential dates?

One friend has a lengthy web page fleshing out many questions woman have wanted to know about him, from his relationship history, to philosophy on money, kids, sex, politics, religion, grooming, etc. He sends the URL to any woman wanting to know about him.

My friend George did a similar thing with his "disclaimer" (see "Sharing your dating disclaimer," in *Iron Out Dating Wrinkles: Work Through Challenges Without Getting Steamed* book) which he shared with women before getting intimate.

A relationship résumé is slightly different than the Boyfriend Application discussed in "Boyfriend application to go with job description." An application tells the "employer" what s/he wants to know about the applicant. But a résumé tells the""employer" what you want him/her to know.

What would you put in your relationship résumé?

What would you put in your relationship résumé — and want in someone else's? Here are a few items off the top of my head.

- 💜 Relationship goal: LTR? Casual dating? Casual intimacy?

- 💜 Age (real age, not "what I think I look/act like" age)

- 💜 Height; build; tattoos; piercings

- 💜 Kids? If yes, ages and living at home?

- 💜 Current marital status; if separated, for how long; if pending divorce, when expected to be divorced; if widowed, since when; if divorced, date of final decree as well as date of initial separation

💜 How long married and how old were you when marriage(s) began.

💜 History of other post-marriage relationships lasting more than a year.

💜 Why relationship(s) broke up. What part you played in the break up. What you learned from the relationship and break up.

💜 What do you want to make sure exists in your next relationship. What do you want to make sure is absent from your next relationship.

💜 Health, including any chronic physical or mental maladies.

💜 Residence status: Own home? Live with room-mates?

💜 Work status: Employed? Title? How long with current employer? Prior to that?

💜 What would you add to a template for a relation-ship résumé?

Are you "skin hungry"?

friend used this term to describe when someone longs for touch. She said it means someone hasn't been touched in a while, or perhaps as much as they like. Maybe their friends or family aren't the touching type. They crave human contact — literally — but especially opposite-sex contact, even if it's just holding hands or hugging.

Although I like physical contact, I've had dates get too touchy too soon. I've tended to think they were just horny, even if they didn't try to read my body using the Braille method.

Have you ever found yourself being a bit physically clingy, especially on the first or second dates, before you really know the guy? I've found myself slipping my hand in his on the second date, before I really felt a lot of connection, just because it seemed like that's what should happen at that point.

So I empathize with someone's wanting physical touch. I've learned to be a tad cautious, however, as we know touch sends signals that you are feeling connected and fond of the person. Sometimes this gets interpreted as feeling more attracted to the person than you are.

What to do when you find yourself being skin hungry? See if you can be around family members who enjoy your touch. Young nieces, nephews or grandkids who like to hold hands or sit in your lap while you read to them are great ways to get your skin hunger satisfied. Or plan an outing with a friend who likes to hug hello or link arms when walking. I have a male friend who loves to snuggle, so going to the movies with him is a treat when I have a touching deficit.

But with your dates, be conscious if your itch to be touched is appropriate to be scratched by him. Be sensitive to the message that it sends. And if the touching goes beyond what you are comfortable with, then gently say something. Don't punish him for a yearning you have that may send him an unintentional green light.

What's your "need for affiliation"?

A gal pal shared with me the concept of people having different needs for affiliation — how much "people contact" they need.

As you would guess, some have a very low need for affiliation — someone like the Unabomber who is content to live like a hermit with human contact only a few times a year, and then only because of necessity. Granted, he is mentally ill, but you get my drift.

And some people have a very high need to be around others and get depressed when they aren't. Think Paris Hilton (we'll skip any assessment about mental health). I find it interesting that some of these folks can just be in the presence of others — not interacting with them — and still have their itch scratched. That may be the case for people who spend all day in a popular park, Starbucks, Borders, or the library, reading and working. They talk with very few people, if any, but they just like being around others.

My theory is this: Your dating behaviors reflect your

need for affiliation. So if you have a high need, you're apt to email, call and IM the person you're dating multiple times a day. (We began to explore this in "Do you both have the same dating rhythm?" in the *In Search of King Charming: Who Do I Want to Share My Throne?* book)

If your guy has less need for affiliation — perhaps much less — than you, he will soon tire of scratching your people-contact itch. But if you think he's just being standoffish, or ignoring you, you will become annoyed.

And if it is he who has the higher people-connection need, you will be irritated about his seemingly unending desire for attention. And "need" is the operative word here. It is the word we use to describe people who want more than we are comfortable giving: needy.

Some people have a very high need to be around others

But what if you both have similar affiliation needs? Then it's not really needy, is it? You're both scratching each other's itch. And it feels good. Or what if you both have high affiliation needs, but he doesn't contact you as often as you'd like because he gets his needs met by coworkers and pals?

So define where you are on an Affiliation Continuum. I know, sometimes it varies. But think, generally, do

you like a lot of people contact, talking to coworkers frequently at work, chatting with friends and family while commuting, exercising and while doing chores? Do you have talk radio on at home, work and/or the car? Is the TV on when you're home, even when you're not watching? Do you IM, text and/or email constantly? Give yourself a 10.

Or, at the other end of the spectrum, do you rarely talk on the phone other than for business? Do your parents have to call you because you don't think of calling them? Would you prefer to get an email over talking on the phone? Is your home silent, or with just instrumental music in the background and the TV rarely on? Are you more likely to read or work in a deserted place, rather than in a public spot with people around?

You could think I'm describing introverts and extroverts. But take a look at these definitions:

- Introvert: a shy, reticent, and typically self-centered person; a person predominantly concerned with their own thoughts and feelings rather than with external things.

- Extrovert: an outgoing, overtly expressive person; a person predominantly concerned with external things or objective considerations.

I see these as different from the need for affiliation. You could be an extrovert — the life of the party — when you are at a party, but not have a strong need to be at a lot of parties. Or you could like to talk on the phone and be around other people without being gregarious, a common description of extroverts.

The point is to be conscious of your need for affiliation and sensitive to his. Mark where you are most comfortable on the Affiliation Continuum between 1 and 10. Place a mark where you think your guy falls. See if you're a long way apart. If so, then discuss it.

For example, if he's a once-a-day-contact guy and you are a multiple-contact gal, then ask if it bothers him that you contact him a few times a day. If he says no, then also say you are perfectly OK with his saying he'll get back to you later if it isn't a good time. The key is to be sensitive to what's driving your behavior, as well as his needs, and try not to be judgmental about his.

But that's the key to so much in having a healthy relationship, isn't it?

Can too much spoiling be bad?

A man contacted me whose online name is the equivalent of Wuss4U. I laughed, as I thought it must be a joke. I read his profile:

> "I seek an aggressive woman who wants to take charge and call the shots. I am meek and mild, shy. I need a strong, forceful woman to dominate me. Tell me where to go and what to do. I will do as you say without any back talk or lip. Age, height, weight are not important. If you are interested, please wink or email me as I am probably too timid to approach you first. I am hoping for a LTR or marriage.
>
> "It would be fun just to be with you. You pick the movie. You control the TV remote. You choose the restaurant. Just let me bask in your presence and serve your desires. Where would you like to go? I will be happy to go with you and look after your needs.

*"My favorite thing is treating you like a princess.
Your pleasure and delight is most important to me."*

Is this a joke? (I realize there is a whole subculture for those interested in dominance/submission. Those people are usually listed on specialized sites, not mainstream ones.) For discussion's sake, let's assume he's serious and not just kinky.

Some men think women want a man to cater to her every whim. To kowtow to her. To be subservient. I know few — if any — women who desire this. This man has taken to extreme a woman's desire to be appreciated and receive attention, and yes, get what she wants equally with doing what he wants. We all desire someone who pays attention to what we like and works to give that to us. It works both ways.

> *Some men think women want a man to cater to her every whim.*

Control issues can be a problem, no matter the gender. What about give-up-control issues? Would you like to be with someone who only cared about what you wanted? Only did what you wanted? On one level it would seem perfect — at least for those who really only want someone to accompany them on their desired outings.

Part of the allure of having a relationship is seeing life from another's perspective, experiencing what gives them joy, and perhaps expanding your own horizons. I know I've enjoyed this part of dating. I like it when men take me into a world I wouldn't have sought to discover on my own. Sometimes I've liked the new experience; sometimes I've said, "Once was enough."

So how would you like being with Wuss4U? Would that be your idea of nirvana or hell?

What's in a name?

ately, I've been contacted by a number of men with formal names: Patrick not Pat, Charles not Charlie or Chuck, Richard not Dick or Rick or Rich. I've also noticed that people who use the formal version of their name are different than those who offer the informal version.

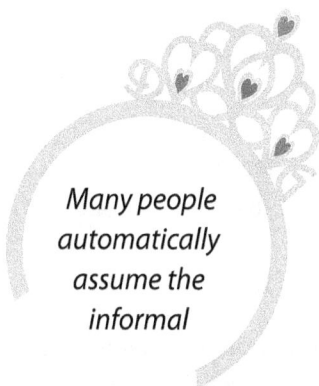

> *Many people automatically assume the informal*

Since I use the formal version of my name and loathe the informal version, I am sensitive to how people call themselves. I notice how someone introduces him/herself and I make a point to call them by that name. Many people automatically assume the informal. If you introduce yourself as Patricia and someone says, "Nice to meet you, Patty" it says a lot about them. They are insensitive to how others prefer to be addressed.

It can backfire, too. I have a friend whose business cards say "Frederick." People who don't know him shorten it to "Fred." But he goes by "Rick." So he knows immediately if someone is trying to seem too chummy too soon.

My ex used his formal name, too. It astounded us to introduce ourselves at a party and hear someone immediately call us the informal versions. With few exceptions, those people did not seem to be astute about other things as well.

I'm not sure I can articulate what it is about people who use the formal versions of their name. They are not better — I don't mean to imply that. They can be down-to-earth, funny, and warm. But there is something different about Bob than Robert, Richard from Dick, Charlie from Chuck.

If I'm in doubt — a man introduces himself as Robert, but then someone calls him Rob — I ask which he prefers. Once I asked a man if he'd like me to call him Mike or Michael. He paused, thinking, then said, "My mother calls me Michael. I'd like you to call me Michael." I was hoping that was a good sign!

If you use the formal version of your name — say, Suzanne or Susan — but a date calls you Suzi or Sue, what do you think that says about him? And if he introduces himself with the formal version, have you noticed a trend with others who also use their formal name?

Even eye candy isn't good if you're allergic

A date and I attended a Halloween party. The room was filled with scantily clad, hard-bodied beautiful people in provocative costumes. I tried to fit in with a comparably sedate, decidedly more understated attempt at a dominatrix. While I felt comfortable in my costume, even with my chubby, fishnet-encased legs flowing from my leather skirt (accented by a whip and name tag stating "Mistress R") I wondered what my date thought of the beautiful, barely dressed women nearby.

> *"That Paris Hilton look alike in the bikini looks cold," I commented.*
>
> *"Yeah. Not too smart to wear that to a party in October."*
>
> *"I bet you'd like to be held captive by that beautiful, stiletto-heeled pirate in the micro-miniskirt," I teased.*
>
> *"Nah. I'd rather walk the plank."*

As we admired the imagination and creativity of

other costumes and how great people looked in them, he said, "They can look good, but based on some of our conversations with them, there doesn't seem to be a lot of substance. I've learned that for me, it's like being in a candy store looking at all the goodies, but then remembering that you're allergic to sugar. Within a nanosecond you realize you aren't interested in anything there."

This was an interesting perspective for me to hear. Based on preferences of the vast majority of men's online profiles, I've generalized that nearly all men would pick the Paris Hilton-type bodies over my curvy one carrying extra pounds. It was reassuring that he didn't find these model-like women to be appealing. And it showed that he was a conscious gentleman to not go ga-ga over these women while with me.

He continued, "Sexiness and appeal have much more to do with how a woman carries herself — her posture, her walk, her dress — than her weight or figure. A woman who knows how to dress to her strengths and is happy with herself is sexy no matter what her size."

I kissed him. I couldn't help myself.

How do you feel about how you carry yourself? Do you think you project happiness and confidence? If not, what could you do to show more self-assuredness?

Advice from sister-surrogate sages

Having lunch with two friends, both 16 years my senior, we were discussing relationships. They asked about my love life, always wanting an update on the soap opera of my dating situation. One had been married nearly 50 years, the other was a divorcée from a 30-year marriage. I often bounced my relationship dilemmas off them.

I shared I was torn between two really great guys, one of whom I'd been seeing for five weeks, the other for three. Both were generous, affectionate, communicative, tender, intelligent, and successful. The 5-week one had also shown he was reliable, thoughtful about pleasing me, and emotionally mature, but I wasn't physically drawn to him. He wasn't unattractive; it was more his kiss and touch didn't do it for me. The 3-week man also displayed some of the same positive characteristics, but since we hadn't spent as much time together, the evidence was less apparent. But I got goose bumps with his touch and kiss. We definitely had chemistry.

I was wondering if it was right to keep seeing the

5-week guy since I didn't have the same physical reaction to him. Was I being fair to him? Would I grow to get excited by his touch? Should I let him loose and focus on the one who got my blood boiling? Or should I continue to see both a bit longer and see if one emerged as the clear front runner?

My two sages offered their input.

The longer-married one began: "After a while, the physical part of a relationship wanes, no matter how hard you try. If you have to choose between a good man and a hot one — at least for the long term — always choose the one who treats you the best. The hottie may be good for a tryst, but sex appeal is not the primary basis on which to build a relationship."

The other chimed in, "Yes, passion fades, but respect, kindness, and emotional maturity are more likely to stay intact. If you're looking to stop dating around and settle down, focus on the one who shows more solid character, even if you're less drawn to him physically."

They wanted an update on the soap opera of my dating situation

"But," I protested, "if I can't get excited about him physically, how will that bode for the relationship? In the beginning if one isn't pulled to a man, can you learn to be passionate toward him?"

"Do you think he's teachable? Could he learn how you like to be kissed and touched?" asked the 50-year veteran.

"Yes, I believe he would want to learn. He does seem interested in pleasing me."

The divorcée added, "You can be swept off your feet by passion. It is exhilarating. But it often blinds us to the lack of other important criteria by which to make a long-term decision. Yes, ideally your future mate and you will have passion for many, many years. But the relationship should be grounded on mutual respect, caring, kindness, and wanting to make each other happy — not only in the bedroom, but in general."

The long-married friend capped the conversation with, "Dear, you've only just begun to get to know these men. You don't have to choose at this juncture. Just enjoy having two great guys in your life, be respectful of their feelings, and when the time is right, it will be clear which one should get your focus. Or maybe neither of these is the right one for you. Have a good time while being mindful of not doing or saying things that make them think you are focused on one exclusively."

These surrogate big sisters served thoughts to chew on as we nibbled our lunch. Having their 80+ years of relationship wisdom in which to marinate my thoughts was the seasoning I was looking for.

Why are we drawn to bad boys?

They are like forbidden foods when we are on a diet. They pull us toward them, no matter how much self-control we try to have. We work to resist, but their beckoning becomes too much for us. We succumb to their wiles.

What is it about bad boys — who are, of course, really midlife men — that is so irresistible to some? Intellectually, you know they are certain trouble. They will say and do the things that melt you. You quickly give them your heart on a silver platter: "Here it is — my heart. Take it. I offer it willingly." Even if you've seen signs that he won't protect it, you serve it to him with little, if any, hesitation.

Is it that they've learned how to address your surface emotional needs? They say all the right things, "Don't ever change. You are perfect the way you are." "I see us together for a long, long time." "Where have you been all my life?" "You're someone I can take home to my mother. She'll love you." "You make me very happy." "I'm afraid

I'm falling for you." I even had one say on the phone to his sister when I walked into the room, "Your future sister-in-law just came in."

It's not just their words. It's their touch, their kiss, how they look at you, with that look that says they are really, really, really into you. It's the pheromones — that chemistry thing, but it's like love potion mixed with steroids.

Are we so needy to hear sweet things that we overlook the parts that aren't good? We want to be in love so desperately that we ignore the clear signs he isn't emotionally mature or available? We

It's like love potion mixed with steroids.

aren't fully emotionally available ourselves so we choose guys who will leave us in the dust as quickly as they stole our hearts? Is it low self-esteem, even when we have high self-esteem in many other areas?

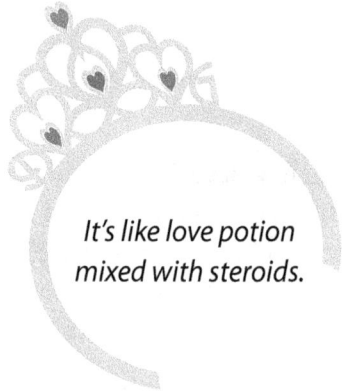

What is it that is so alluring? Have they figured out how to hypnotize us? They know what many women want from a man? That they can love us and leave us and we'll still long for them to return with open arms?

What's your theory — or experience — with the temptations of bad boys? Why do we fall for them so readily? Even when we're at midlife and know better?

Where are you on the relationship recovery path?

dventures in Delicious Dating After 40 reader
Devon wrote:

> All divorced people are in a different place along
> the post-divorce road. I met someone wonderful
> last summer, attraction, chemistry, great sex, good
> conversation and we had fun. It lasted 3 months, I
> was ready for a companion, he was still recovering
> from the break up of his family and the stress of a
> recent divorce. After 4 years of being single I have
> a different outlook and want something different
> than a newly divorced man. I wonder if anyone
> has put a name to the stages of recovery from
> divorce, there must be similar things people go
> through. I would guess we all go through a redis-
> covery of (good) sex.
>
> Some of the men I've dated might have been keep-
> ers if the timing had been better. Since the healing
> process is different for everyone the whole thing is
> rather unpredictable. Any thoughts?

Good point, Devon. Yes, I think there are stages of recovery after a the end of an important relationship. However, it can be hard to identify where you are in your own recovery, let alone determine someone else's. Here are some steps on the path.

First, you need to grieve the loss of the relationship and your life with your ex. If you jump too soon into a new relationship, you aren't fully available to be with a new person.

The path includes admitting how you contributed — even a bit — to the decline of the relationship, even if he treated you hideously. If you don't look at why you got into or stayed in a dysfunctional relationship, you're doomed to repeat the same pattern until you identify your part and work to heal it.

Once you are healed, you learn (if you hadn't already) how to enjoy time by yourself without needing a man in your life. Once you are centered and happy, you can choose to open your heart to another and begin dating. If you start before this point, you will be frustrated and disappointed about the men who you attract to you. Even after this point, you may still attract men who are not good matches. But it's all part of the process if you learn from it and don't make judgments about "all men are jerks, cads, sex crazed, etc."

What are your thoughts on the relationship recovery path? Are there steps missing in the above? What would you add? How do you know where you are on the path — or how to tell where someone else is?

The man-sieve

Unless you live in a remote area, there are eligible, age-appropriate single men all around you. You have developed a filter for either attracting them or not, or accepting or rejecting date requests.

Before you began dating you may have said, "I don't really know what I want, so I'll go out with anyone who asks." Your "man-sieve" has small holes and catches many men.

Or you set abundant criteria a man must meet before you'll consider going out with him. Your man-sieve is loosely meshed, with large holes, allowing all but a very few to pass through.

As you date a few men, you adjust the man strainer. If you meet too many men who don't meet your minimum criteria, you loosen your sieve so more fall through, only allowing the ones who are a likely match to be caught.

Or if you find nearly no one meets your expectations, you realize you are being unrealistic and you allow a few more to be caught. Maybe rather than insisting a man be 6-feet tall you go out with 5-foot-11 or 5-foot-10 ones. Or rather than turning down anyone who doesn't have a 4-year college degree, you look for intelligence, articulateness, and worldliness, even though he left Harvard mid-way, à la Bill Gates.

Have you examined your man-sieve lately? We often do so after a particularly odious date — "I've got to develop better criteria for who I'll go out with." Eventually you come upon a good mix of must-haves with nice-to-haves. You refine your filter so you are only going out with men who are good potential matches.

What have you noticed about how you've adjusted your man sieve over time? Have you tightened or loosened your criteria — or perhaps some of both?

Are you angry with him — or yourself?

Lately I've noticed myself getting angry with men I'm getting to know. The causes can be varied: he doesn't call when he says he will, he doesn't call for weeks then acts like we talked yesterday, he gets too fresh too soon, he doesn't honor my stated boundaries, he makes assumptions without checking them out with me.

I hear myself saying — generally in my mind afterward — "You can't treat me like that." Sometimes I speak up in the moment, but sometimes I don't know how to say what's on my mind without sounding accusatory. Or sometimes I haven't articulated my feelings or thoughts until after the incident.

It is easy, I notice, to blame him: "How dare he..," "How could he...," "How could he think that what he said/did would be acceptable?"

However, the more I mull over what happened and who's to blame, I notice the blaming fingers go in both directions. Yes, a midlife man should know .... But if you've dated only a few women after your 20-year marriage dissolved, your "appropriateness" gauge might be a little rusty. Perhaps I'm giving men more slack than they are due.

But let's give them this slack for a moment. We can come back to vilifying them later. ☺

When I look at the situations, even when I spoke up, I am complicit in the problem. I am really angry at myself — at least in part — for not being more firm in my boundaries, not voicing my expectations up front of what was and wasn't acceptable, or not immediately saying, "That's not cool," or "We're not going there," or "I'm not ready for …." Most of my midlife women pals are assertive, clear and confident communicators, but we can also send mixed messages. Women are socialized to not make waves, to foster peace and harmony, to not make anyone feel bad.

All of these attributes can be positive in the right circumstances. But they can also be detrimental — especially if the man is manipulative or abusive. When we don't stand up for what we want, we get angry. Usually that anger is focused on the other person. But we should accept that part of that anger should be at ourselves for not taking a stand for what we want.

Have you noticed upon reflection that your anger, at least in part, is caused by something you should have said or did but didn't? How have you learned to not take all the blame, nor blame it all on him, but to share it?

Do you like yourself better now?

" **I** like you better now than when you were married," a professional acquaintance shared recently.

It was a surprising statement from someone I didn't know well. But it got me thinking. How am I different than I was 5 years ago when my ex left? What has caused the change? Do I like me more now?

As I reflected on his comment and my answers to the questions, I realized I was different. How am I different in ways this colleague might notice, since he only sees me twice a year at our professional association meetings? I think I am more playful and flirtatious. I'm willing to wear sexier attire at our formal events. I think I smile more and am less uptight.

Not that being married would preclude any of those behaviors. But I think the divorce caused me to intensely reflect on my behaviors. Then going through the dating gauntlet repeatedly and learning that more often than not the men I meet find me attractive has given me a new confidence. I was always confident professionally, but I didn't feel especially attractive to men other than my husband when I was married, and I didn't welcome opportunities to find out if I was.

I've noticed many people are bitter after a divorce or LTR breakup. They are unhappy and it shows through their body language, dress and attitude. They don't feel attractive so they aren't. They could be good looking but their demeanor telegraphs ugliness. They aren't attracting anyone. Which makes them more bitter: "There aren't any good men/women out there," "All the good ones are taken."

Are you more attractive now, even if you have the same haircut, wear the same clothes, and are in the same shape as before? If you've worked through your hurt, anger and/or guilt, you likely have a lighter, happier facial expression, stand straighter and exude

They are unhappy and it shows through their body language, dress and attitude

openness. You may smile or laugh more often or more quickly. You make eye contact longer. You may even perceive yourself differently and try a new haircut, new clothes style or exercise more.

If you don't like yourself better now, why not? Do you feel you have to be in a loving, committed relationship to be happy? Can't you be happy and then a loving relationship will just make you happier?

You are the only person who can make you happy or unhappy. If you don't like something about yourself, then focus on changing it. No one will ever be completely happy with all aspects of themselves, but if we are intent on improving, we can't help liking ourselves more now than in the past.

Have you considered how you are different than when you were last in a long-term relationship? If someone you hadn't seen since then were to spend time with you now, what would they notice is different? If you are different, what caused the change? And most importantly, do you like yourself better now?

Make peace with your body parts

idlife women have shared with me that they didn't want to start dating until they lost weight and/or got in shape. Some said the thought of getting undressed in front of a man was so unnerving, they would rather not start the dating process if that was to be the end result. In "Getting naked with him the first time" I talked about the experience of being unclothed with someone for the first time.

But today I want to explore what you can do to be at peace with any of your body "particulars" with which you have some issues and that are preventing you from moving forward in the dating process.

A few years ago I took a weekend course on women's body esteem from Rita Hovakimian. In it, she had us do a powerful exercise designed to help us stop being critical of body parts we weren't fond of.

Let's say you are critical of your thighs, calling them "thunder thighs," and being upset with their size, shape and lack of tone. You've blamed their shape on your mother's genes and have diligently exercised to try to reduce their size and get them into the long, slender shape you desire. However, no matter what you do they continue to maintain their chubby appearance.

Rita had each workshop participant change into tights and leotards or a bathing suit and have a conversation with these less-than-ideal body parts, as if they were a separate person. So, the conversation with my thighs went like this:

Rita: How do you feel about your thighs?

Me: I'm disgusted with them. They are big and flabby and cellulite riddled. I wish I could just cut off the flab.

Rita: Okay. Let's ask your thighs how they feel about your thinking this about them.

Me: (As my thighs) We are sad that you dislike us so much. We do a lot for you. We help you walk, bike, dance and exercise. We enabled you to ski for years. And now all we hear is complaints. How about some acknowledgment for what we do for you?

Rita: What do you think about that?

Me: They are right. I only focus on what I don't like.

Rita: What can you sincerely acknowledge about your thighs? Tell them.

Me: Thighs, thank you for being so strong and powerful. You enable me to ride my bike, dance, do aerobics, walk, and hike. I appreciate the years of pleasure you've allowed me to have from these activities. You've never let me down.

Rita: Thighs, how do you feel hearing that?

Thighs: It feels great to be appreciated. We feel loved.

Rita: Your thighs have served you, even in their larger-than-you'd-like current form. They have done their job for you without fail. Can you forgive that they don't have your ideal shape and allow them to continue to do their job, and appreciate them for it?

Me: Absolutely.

The thought of getting undressed in front of a man was unnerving

Rita: Thighs, how does it feel to hear that?

Thighs: Great. And we only got big to get some attention. If we got more regular love an acknowledgment, we wouldn't need to be quite so big.

Me: I will love you no matter what your size.

Within months of this process, with the help of exercise, my thighs were a bit more slender and toned. They are still not my ideal shape, but I have let go of my loathing of them.

So I've given up being concerned about what a guy will think upon seeing them for the first time. If he's disapproving, he's not for me. And I can tell if he's going to be critical of me and my body particulars long before he sees me unclothed, so I stop seeing him as I don't need judgmental people in my life.

Do you have some body parts with which you need to make peace and appreciate so you can progress in dating? Try a conversation similar to the above and see what comes out. You may be surprised.

The zest test

An attractive, successful, intelligent, sexy 48-year-old man told me on our first date that he'd only had two other dates in the last 3.5 years. I asked why.

"I'm not attracted to most women."

This was unusual, as I'd heard that many men are attracted to a lot of women who meet their physical criteria. So I probed.

"What are most women lacking that make you not attracted to them?"

He thought for a moment. "A zest for life. Gusto. Joie de vivre. Most of the women I talk to are complaining about something — exes, bosses, money, their bodies, men, life. It sucks the wind out of me. A beautiful woman complaining is suddenly unattractive. But an attractive woman who is upbeat, positive and fun becomes stunningly beautiful. It's very much part of your allure to me."

I was flattered. I hadn't really thought about my attitude and how it compared to other women. Since I hang out with positive, upbeat people, when I encounter negative complainers I high-tail it out of the situation as quickly as possible. So I understood what he was talking about. But I found it interesting that he found so many women were down about life.

It reminded me how important those first encounters are with a new person. Not that you should be obsessively guarded about what you say, but I think we should be conscious of the impression we're giving. If you have challenges, it's OK to share them, but not on the first date or two. Save them for a little later, if you have any interest in seeing the guy again.

Early on in my post-divorce dating life I hadn't quite figured this out. I remember scratching my head after several first dates I thought went well, then I got the "we're not a match" email afterward. Looking back on the conversations, I noticed

We should be conscious of the impression we're giving

a trend. We would swap stories about our exes, both of us complaining about how or why the ex left. I thought we were bonding through commiseration. I think part of why there wasn't an attraction is that complaining is rarely attractive — even if you both seem to be doing an equal amount of it. You'd think complainers would band together — and sometimes they do. But I don't think it's good date behavior.

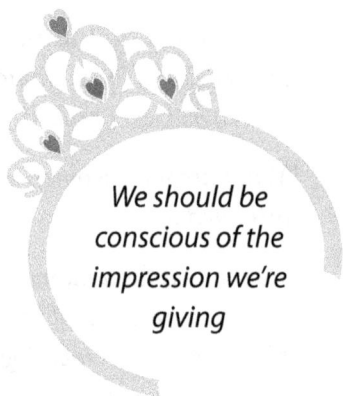

So before a first date, think about the things in life for which you have passion. If need be, make a list. When it's your turn to share, talk about what excites you. Even if it something that holds no interest for him, it's hard to be bored when someone is expressing their passion. If he shows some interest in your topic, great. Ask what he's passionate about, as well. Very few people are asked that question and it will show you're focused on positives.

Do you feel you have zest? If so, how do you express it?

Cultivate and appreciate your band of brothers

There's a group of guys who are like my brothers. You probably have some male friends like that, too. My chosen chums have become closer to me than my biological brother.

You'll probably find that your buds stick with you through your dating adventures. Some want to hear how it went after you meet a new guy. Some help you understand the male perspective when you're flummoxed. Others provide a comforting shoulder to cry on after a particularly painful encounter.

Most of my bro's are protective. They tell me to warn a suitor that if he does me wrong, he'll have to deal with them. Some want to check out any new potential long-term love to make sure he's good enough for me and will treat me right. I was touched when my ex's brother called him on the carpet after leaving me. His own brother lambasted him for leaving me! How cool is that?

Having pals – both guys and gals – helps you feel that you're not in this dating game alone. Yes, gal pals provide counsel as well as solace. But knowing you have male compadres who are looking out for you can give you peace of mind.

If you don't have a bevy of buds, perhaps some would step to the plate if you asked their opinion on something. I've been amazed at how friendly acquaintances have become comrades just by my asking them about how men think. They are flattered you asked and can become a cheerleader and confidant.

Who are your adopted brothers? Let them know you appreciate their support.

Are you a happy dater?

A friend asked me how I managed to stay so happy without yet finding The One. It's true that generally I'm a perpetually perky person, but I do have my bouts with unhappiness when faced with setbacks and disappointments. I've worked hard to reduce the time I spend in a dreary mood when something unpleasant happens. Or if something I'd looked forward to doesn't materialize. I like to think of myself as the Lemonade Queen, quickly making the quenching drink out of life's lemons.

A man I talked with nightly for three weeks was also generally upbeat, rarely complaining about anything — including his divorce or ex — even after the dozen hours we've spent talking. It is compelling and refreshing and shows a positive outlook on life. It made me think about what attracts us to others. He shared that this was one of the reasons he was drawn to me — I seemed to possess an endless good mood.

Contrast this to another man I talked with daily for months who seemed to be continually complaining about something: traffic, his job, his coworkers, his golf game, the weather, his son, his ex, his parents. After a kvetch session I asked him, "What do you like about your job?" He said, "There's plenty I like about my job." I responded, "I don't hear about what you like very often." While it's important to recruit a vent buddy, if you haven't agreed to that role it can get wearisome if someone goes on and on only complaining.

I once attended a seminar that encouraged: "Don't complain unless it's to someone who can do something about it." This negates the common advice that you should vent to someone so you feel better. I think a better approach is to not inflict that negative energy on anyone else. If you need to release, sit in your car and let loose. Or write out your frustration. Or if you do

It can get wearisome if someone only complains

choose to vent with a pal, make sure it is less than 10% of your conversation, and first ask him/her if it is OK to vent for 5 minutes.

It's easy to get frustrated dating and want to vent. After all my dating not resulting in "The One," I could focus on what was wrong with all of the men I've dated. But that wouldn't help keep me in the hunt with a positive mind set. Sometimes you have to make your own happiness in the face of what others would think would be demoralizing.

In "I'm glad dating is hard" (see the *Date or Wait: Are You Ready for Mr. Great?* book) I mentioned my friend the late Art Berg. While in rehab after a partially paralyzing spinal cord injury (SCI), his doctor kept sending psychiatrists to see him. Art thought it was odd that he was sequestered from other SCI patients. Later, in examining his medical records, he found the reason noted by his doctor: "Excessive happiness." The doctor felt he laughed too much and was in too good of a mood much of the time. While the doctor thought this was a detriment to his recovery as he interpreted this as denial, Art said it was key to his recovery and subsequent success in life.

Here's Art's recipe for excessive happiness:

- Happiness is a choice — a choice we make every day.

- Happiness is not a condition of our circumstances or external influences. It is a state of mind and heart.

- Happiness comes most often when we focus on solving other people's pain and problems as opposed to thinking only of our own.

- Happiness isn't what we have or who we are. It's feeling valuable and worthy regardless of our station in life.

- Happiness is within everyone's reach.

Are you a happy dater? Perhaps an excessively happy one? If so, how do you keep yourself up amid rejection and disappointment?

Give yourself more dating happiness

Let's take a look at how we can meld things that make us happy into our dating activities. Start by looking at simple pleasures that make you happy. Here are some of mine:

- Sitting in and working in my garden
- Reading an interesting book
- Watching an interesting movie
- Napping
- Biking
- Hiking
- Watching the ocean
- Snorkeling
- Viewing a thought-provoking museum exhibit
- People watching
- Chocolate!

- ♥ Meaningful discussions
- ♥ Listening to and/or dancing to R&B music
- ♥ Warm bubble bath
- ♥ Silk, cashmere, suede
- ♥ Comfortable shoes
- ♥ Cute shoes
- ♥ Cute, comfortable shoes
- ♥ Stretching/yoga
- ♥ Laughing/making others laugh

Now the key is to see how many you can combine with your date. I can do all of the above alone or with someone. When you make your list, see which ones you can enjoy with a special guy.

Now you may think this is common sense. I used to think the same way. Until I noticed I was doing most of the above alone or with gal pals. Now I'm better at suggesting activities from the above list, as well as participating in things from his list. If you only suggest or agree to the traditional movies and dinner, it gets old, even if you like that as an evening's entertainment. Mix it up.

You could ask the guy you're seeing to make his list, you make yours, then you show each other your lists and see which ones you are interested in doing together. It will make you happier to be together!

My list also included:

💜 Flirting with an interesting guy

💜 Hugs

💜 Kisses

💜 Snuggling

Which, of course, I can also do with a special guy!

Decide to make yourself happy

If you're dating someone you aren't happy around, decide to make yourself happy or get out now. Notice I didn't say "someone who doesn't make you happy." You, of course, are the only one who can make yourself happy or unhappy. But sometimes we think we are looking for someone who will make us happy. And I do think it's important to be with someone who's interested in making you happy. But ultimately, it is you who decides if you are happy or not.

Making your own happiness

Yesterday was my birthday. When your birthday approaches, do you ask yourself, "What do I want?" Not just tangible presents, but what would make you happy not only on that day, but in life? I do.

Approaching my birthday, I decided I wanted to spend it with King Charming. Since I didn't expect him to intuit what I wanted, I thought of several experiences I could suggest that would make me happy:

- going dancing
- having drinks on the patio of a favorite restaurant at sunset
- hiking through a local park to admire the wildflowers
- a drive and overnight through a picturesque part of our area
- dinner at a local fondue restaurant
- going to a comedy club

There was only one problem: my beau was out of town and not to return until after my birthday. So what would be Plan B that would still make me happy?

Gal pals.

Thank heavens for our gal pals. A common complaint when a woman goes ga ga for a man is that their gal pals are neglected. However, they are the ones who will be there through it all, good and bad, from sublime smitten through bawling breakup. Don't ignore them. Mine came through like champs and I celebrated for 4 days thanks to the generosity of fabulous women who I don't get to spend much time with as they live several hours away.

> *Gal pals will be there from sublime smitten through bawling breakup*

One invited me to her forest home to relax (she has a heated pool, hot tub, sauna, and home theater) and do a little work on each other's business. We interspersed this with hiking, talking about life, watching a DVD and, of course, laughing. We helped each other craft breakthroughs in our businesses.

A close gourmet friend allowed me to invite myself to dinner when passing through her town. Her sumptuous Italian feast was preceded with a hike through a local mountain park.

After dinner, I drove to another's home and we talked until late, then I crashed. She treated me to a great breakfast as her 2.5-year-old cherubic daughter entertained me.

And to cap the birthday tour, I'd invited another dear gal pal to accompany me to fondue dinner. She arranged for balloons and chocolate souvenirs — but the cute waiter was a bonus!

So I got hikes, views, fondue, fun, great conversation — and chocolate!

Sometimes we look to the men we're dating to supply the bulk of our happiness. However, most of us know how to create our own happiness without a man. If we've been single for long, we've had to or else we suffer with "If only I had a boyfriend who would…." That's just silly.

Was I disappointed that my beau would not be around? Of course. But you can't let disappointments stop you from getting what you want.

What would make you happy — with or without a man? Start putting it in motion now.

Are your conversational habits costing you dates?

I vet potential dates via the phone before meeting. Why? Because if I don't enjoy the conversation on the phone, it's pretty much guaranteed I won't enjoy the face-to-face. I know some people are uncomfortable on the phone, but in this day and age, if you can't converse comfortably whether on the phone or in person, you're not for me. In the last week I've had four potential suitors call me. Only one received an invitation for a repeat conversation.

Being a conscious conversationalist is critical to a long-term relationship — at least for me. Since I've encountered so many people who are conversationally challenged, I'm assuming it is as much of an issue for women as it is for the men I vet. Since it is doubtful your friends will volunteer that you are an inept conversationalist, as a public service I thought I'd delineate some of the most common conversational culprits.

♥ *Taking most of the air time.* A conscious conversationalist will be aware of approximately how much of the talk time she is taking and when it begins to feel like they've monopolized the conversation, turn the focus on the other person. If you don't know much about the other person, you can simply say, "I've been talking non stop, and I really want to know about you. Tell me something that's new or exciting in your life."

♥ *Repeating yourself.* If you aren't paying enough attention to what you are saying that you repeat yourself, how much do you think the other person will feel you're listening to them?

♥ *Turning the focus back to you.* Last night a new potential suitor called. He regularly turned the conversation to himself. We were talking about the world's awareness of US affairs. Since I hadn't shared much by this point, I said "When I was in Malaysia last summer, I was amazed at how many of my contacts watched the Democratic convention on CNN." His next line was not, "What did you make of that?" or "What did they think of US politics?" or "What were you doing in Malaysia?" No. It was, "A friend has a manufacturing plant in Malaysia that makes dolls. He wants to hire me to do some work for him. Look it up at www.XXXXX.com."

💜 *Not asking relevant follow-up questions.* This same caller said he thought I was fascinating. Which I found odd because I had said barely 10 sentences after 30 minutes into the call. He could have found out about me by asking relevant follow-up questions to my comments, as I illustrated above. If both parties merely jump into a conversation with their own stories or thoughts, it's as if two people are having sequential monologues. To really get to know someone's thoughts, values, and opinions, you have to dig deeper into what they share.

💜 *Delving into unimportant details.* Your conversation partner doesn't need to know every detail of your story. Try to keep it pithy but still include relevant information. Most people could cut their chatter by half, if not 2/3 if they focused on just key elements to get their thought across. If someone wants more detail they'll ask. Better to error on the side of pithiness.

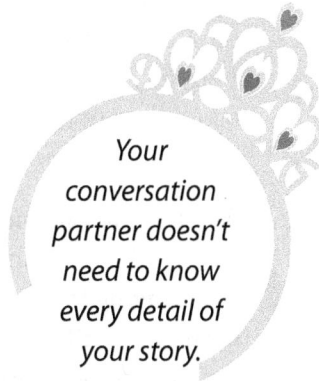

> *Your conversation partner doesn't need to know every detail of your story.*

Interrupting. When someone is talking, let them finish their story or thought. Of course, this is a challenge if they are going on and on and on about something of no interest to you. If you need to interrupt to clarify something, do so with, "I need to interrupt before you go on because I'm confused about…" You are interrupting to better understand what they are sharing, not to change the subject or focus the conversation back on you.

Not letting the other person answer your questions. If you ask a question and as soon as your conversation partner starts sharing, you interject, "That happened to me, too! Let me tell you about it…" you are showing you don't really care to know about them.

Too many non sequiturs. If you can't stay with the thread of the conversation and are continually changing the subject (often back to focusing on you), it is difficult to have an in-depth discussion. Yes, we all get reminded of something that is a little off the subject, and if you find your stream of consciousness takes you far afield, you can acknowledge that, "This is a tad off topic, but your comment reminded me of…." Or if you have more to share on the topic but your partner has gone on a tangent, simply say, "I had another thought I wanted to share on xxx…."

❤ *Short or curt answers.* While I believe in being pithy, curt or short answers are not attractive. If you don't want to talk about something, simply say, "I'd rather not go there right now." or "I'll tell you about that after we've gotten to know each other a bit better."

❤ *Being unaware of what might be of interest to the listener.* If you babble about things your listener probably doesn't care about, then they lose interest not only in the conversation, but with developing a relationship with you. If your side of the dialog is filled with information about your children, grandchildren, first job, high school, your friends (and your friends' children and grandchildren), you'll soon lose your listener. Try to edit in your mind before spewing out whatever crosses your thoughts. Think, "Would this likely interest my listener?" and delete anything that you can't say yes to, no matter how much interest it holds for you. Once someone knows and cares about you, they are more interested in the broader spectrum of your life. But not at first.

❤ *Boasting.* If you are the hero of every story, it gets tedious to listen to you. If you are proud of something, you can start off with, "I'm so excited…" But to keep interjecting stories where you are the champion will earn you the title of bore.

💜 *Name dropping incessantly.* This same caller told me how he had put up a Facebook page and a bunch of politicians had asked to be his friend. He named the politicians, none of whom I recognized. If you have to name drop regularly to show how important you are, you're really telegraphing your insecurities.

We all have some poor conversational habits, myself included. The key is to get some honest feedback from those who care about you. Ask them to be candid with you. Show them the above list and ask if you are guilty of any of the items. And engage them to help you increase your awareness by saying something like "TMI (too much information)" if you start to go into unimportant details.

This will yield not only stronger friendships, but more dates with men who appreciate good conversation!

Do you own your wonderfulness?

In *A Woman's Worth*, Marianne Williamson says, "No man can convince a woman she's wonderful, but if she already believes she is, his agreement can resonate and bring her joy."

But how many of us dating in midlife focus on our wonderful qualities? Isn't it more prevalent to notice your wrinkles, bad habits and other imperfections?

In a recent interview, I was asked "What qualities must a woman over 50 possess in order to maneuver through the dating maze?" I responded, "First, optimism. Really believing you are a great catch and there is someone who will recognize that. Too many women only focus on their flaws, not their characteristics that make them fabulous."

Recently talking to a dating 50+ gal pal, we discussed how easy it is to wonder who would want a woman of our age when there are so many pert young women trolling for men in our age range. My friend is fabulous — smart, thoughtful, attractive, fit, funny, self-aware and accomplished. It's hard to imagine she sees herself as anything but amazing. Yet self-doubt can creep into our psyches, no matter how the outside world sees us.

Marianne Williamson is right — we can't be convinced by an outside source that we are wonderful. It has to come from within. I think others can help us see positive characteristics that we take for granted, so either don't see or ignore. However, if we don't have some seed of self-value, no matter how many times someone tells us how marvelous we are, we'll never believe it.

One of the best gifts we can give to other daters — whether they be pals or someone who interests us — is to sincerely comment on their positive attributes. Even those traits we think they must hear about all the time — their smartness, wittiness, humor, good looks, dependability — still merit an acknowledgment.

Even if someone doesn't think they posses the quality you see, if they hear it often enough the kernel of acceptance will grow. If they hear enough times, they can start to believe it and their confidence will grow.

Being "all that"

In high school, if a girl is described as thinking she's "all that" she's considered arrogant, conceited, stuck up, snobbish. She thinks she's God's gift to the world. She's too good for mere mortals.

Yet, when a young man describes a young woman as "all that" it's a high compliment. He's saying she's sexy, attractive, desirable.

In midlife, do you exude the positive aspects of "all that"? Do you walk with your head high, straight posture, confident? Do you dress flatteringly — age appropriate, neat and well put together? Do you make easy eye contact, have a friendly facial expression?

Of course, the challenge is not to appear conceited, although my observation is that many more women behave less confident than arrogant.

The key is to feel confident, not just pretend. There are those who say "fake it 'til you make it" but I think that is short lived. You need to think of your many positive qualities. Before going out in public, tell yourself to stand tall. Make a practice of looking in the eye anyone who speaks to you. Get in the habit of smiling when you are walking.

You will create an inviting aura. People will smile back at you, say hello, and give you great service. You'll look like someone who knows who she is and what she wants. Men find this appealing (at least healthy, sane men do).

Positive "all that" means you can be humble and self-deprecating, but with confidence. Sound contradictory? When a strong person shows vulnerability it is powerful.

When have you felt "all that" in a positive way? What self-talk enabled you to exude this presence? How did people react to you?

How to be hot

No, I am not going to tell you to wear low-cut tops, skin-tight clothes nor mini-skirts. Although that is hot on some women for some men. But that's not the tip I want to tell you.

I'm going to share something I've stumbled on in my dating adventure. It may be old hat to you. I've been surprised at how universal the effect is on most men, even married pals.

> *I've been surprised at how universal the effect is on most men.*

First, though, you may think it odd for me, a woman who is far from svelte to be sharing a tip on how to be hot. But part of the coolness of this tip is that it works with nearly any body type. I've learned that "hot" has less to do with one's body but more with how one carries oneself.

That's not the tip. But it's part of it.

People most often list "confidence" as a quality they

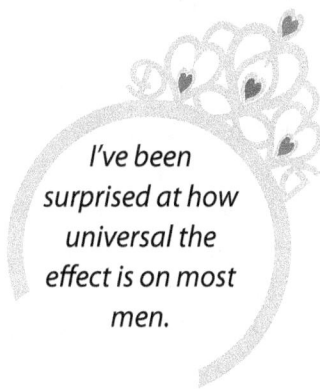

want in a mate. Many men find women sexy who have good posture, a confident walk, look them in the eye, smile easily and speak assuredly. If a woman also dresses like she likes her body — no matter what its size and shape — many men find that appealing. In fact, a hint of cleavage is much more seductive to many men than showing a lot. A 6-inch slit in the front of a skirt showing just a little thigh is much more enticing to many men than a mini-skirt or a high slit.

But the tip I want to share is most appealing when combined with all of the last paragraph. I've gotten the most "you're hot" comments from pals and dates when I've worn … patterned hose. I had no idea this was such a turn on to men!

Tasteful, large-paned fishnet-type hose rarely goes unnoticed. You can have subtle fishnets, stripes, lace or herringbone, but the bolder the pattern the better — at least on the hotness meter. But don't go into garish, wild colors and patterns — those reduce hotness. Men also seem to really like hosiery with a seam up the back, as long as your skirt is above the knee so they can see and appreciate that sexy seam.

But patterned hose on a slouching, timid, dowdily dressed woman isn't alluring. Men have told me that it takes a confident woman to wear patterned hose that calls attention to her legs. And it doesn't seem to really matter the shape of your legs — within reason. I have muscular calves and chubby thighs. This doesn't curtail the comments. But I'm not wearing mini-skirts, either.

So, if you don't already own at least one pair of patterned hosiery, get to the store or online and order a pair. Stand up straight, smile, and feel even more sexy. Tell me how it works for you.

Butt envy

unk in the trunk. Flat. Round. Taut. Soft. Sagging. Dimpled. Some have shelves on the top, others underneath. You could bounce a quarter off a few. So many sizes and shapes.

Songs have been written about buns. "Baby's got back" is a high compliment in some circles.

People can be derrière devotees. Caboose connoisseurs. Ass aficionados.

So much so that they mention their preferences in their dating profiles. I'm told some women feature their keister in their profile pics.

I had an epiphany about rumps in exercise class the other day. Being tall, I purposefully stand near the back. Which opens up a sea of keisters jiggling — or not — before me. I observe, like a scientist, the various sizes, shapes and textures.

Unless you've seen photos of your behind, most of us have only a rough sense of how our tush looks to others. We know if it is large or small, flat or round, but most of this assessment is from the side or at an awkward angle. Unless you have a 3-way mirror in your house, you only occasionally see your heinie the way others do when you are in a store dressing room.

Many of us don't think about our bum a lot, unless we're trying on a new garment or have a hard time zipping pants that fit fine when you wore them a few months ago. The common question, "Do these make my butt look big?" is posed because we are concerned about how we look from the back, and have few opportunities to see for ourself.

I've heard women say a man isn't attractive because he had "no butt." A friend dated his last girlfriend largely because she had junk in her trunk. I find it interesting that a body part that we seldom see for ourself has such allure to others.

Do you find yourself drawn to specific posterior types? So much so that your fondness overshadows other characteristics? Or have you been turned off by less or more in the buns department? Do you feel your own tushie is a liability or an asset?

Have you developed deal-breaker habits?

I once read a study's findings that men who were married/partnered in midlife and older lived longer than men who weren't. The researchers explanation? That if a man has a physical ailment, he'll let it go, not wanting to see a doctor, thinking it will clear up on it's own. If he lives with a woman who knows about the malady, she insists (nags?) him to see the doctor. Thus, ailments that would get worse in time are nipped in the bud and healed.

As we get older, many of us develop bad habits (like thinking something will clear up on its own). If we live by ourselves, or with a non-friend or non-relative roommate, or have friends that aren't very forthcoming to give us feedback, it's easy to start doing things that are unacceptable to others but we think are normal.

This is why some people are in the "undateable" category, no matter how smart or nice they may be.

For example, an older friend has decided she no longer needs to wear deodorant since she mostly just watches TV all day. However, her relatives say being cooped up in a car with her for even short trips requires they roll down the windows because of her BO. Others decide they no longer need to shower every day, or they wear their clothes a day or two longer than they would if someone were around to point out the smell.

It's not just personal hygiene that can fall prey to bad habits. It can be talking to oneself, which isn't a problem when one is alone. But when in the presence of another, constant chattering can cause the other to continually ask you to repeat or speak up, when you were really only thinking aloud. This can be annoying to both of you, yet you're not conscious that you're babbling semi-audibly.

Or perhaps your housekeeping has been lax since it's just you at home now. But when your sweetie visits, he has to step gingerly around the dog food you spilled days ago and haven't gotten around to sweeping up. Or he has to wash a glass for water because all the glassware is in the sink/dishwasher. Or your beloved dog's hair has matted on the couch so he has to endure fur on his black slacks or cover the couch with a dog-smelling throw.

Maybe your habits have spilled over into your table manners. Since you're used to eating alone, you've become oblivious to your chewing with your mouth open, slurping your drink, smacking your lips, or wiping your nose with the cloth napkin. Or since no one checks your tip, you've begun to leave less and less and now think 5% is acceptable.

The list could go on. None of these on their own are deal breakers, but the cumulative affect is that you are unconscious of how your behaviors appear to others.

The cure? I wish adults would more easily enroll in charm or etiquette school, but once one is past school age, few find that acceptable. And it wouldn't address some of the issues listed above.

So how do you know if you have a habit that could be off putting? My suggestion is to seek input from those you trust to tell you the truth and who have some savvy about these things. I wouldn't ask a pal who sees nothing wrong with a sinkload of dishes and rampant dust bunnies to assess your housekeeping habits.

What bad habits have you identified in yourself that needed fixing? Or have you had to tell a sweetheart s/he needs to become aware of a habit that has passed the acceptable range?

Don't let extra pounds slow you down

A reader wrote:

"I am overweight — not morbidly obese but over-weight. I mention in my profile that I am a bit overweight. I have yet to progress from one initial email with anyone. I feel as if it is impossible to get a date with anyone when you are overweight — am I wrong? Should I not mention it and lie like everyone else? This is so frustrating."

First, I'm glad you're honest in your profile. I've met for coffee too many men who listed themselves as "ath-letic" or "average" when they were 80 pounds overweight. I think honesty is important.

However, you can safely say "a few extra pounds" in your profile and people know that means 10-30 pounds. If you say "big and beautiful" that usually means over 50 pounds extra.

The best way is to post a recent, full-length pic of you in something that is flattering. Many men have a shape they are attracted to, even if that shape has extra padding.

You ask if it's impossible to get a date with anyone when you're overweight. I am a living example that you can — in fact, men will not only go out with you, but will find you attractive and sexy. It's not so much the pounds, but how you dress to play up your strengths and how you stand and walk. If you move with confidence, many will overlook some larger-than-normal curves.

If you don't know how to do this, make an appointment with a personal shopper in a store that has your size clothing. Tell her you're starting to date and buy one outfit in which you feel attractive. Also visit the makeup counter and tell the rep you want a new, updated look as you're starting to date. Tell your hair stylist you want something that makes you look and feel cute and sexy.

Knowing that some men like larger women, join a site like www.bbwpersonalsplus.com or www.largeandlovely.com. You may be surprised by how much attention you get if you post attractive photos.

Don't let extra pounds get in the way of your dating life. It hasn't slowed me down and you don't have to either.

What have you done to not let something you feel could be a liability get in the way of your dating life?

The long march toward a valentine

Our society drowns us in Valentine's Day propaganda — cramming down our throats that if we have a sweetie we have to go all out to show our ardor. And by implication, if you don't have a honey, you are a loser.

You know you're not a loser. You have been working toward finding a compatible, mutually attractive sweetheart. You've been consciously and consistently making yourself the best you can be.

You've kept up your beloved-finding activities. Over and over. Like a long march toward an elusive love. You keep at it.

One foot in front of the other.

You keep on trucking.

You plod along.

The search, as with any long trek, is punctuated with highs and lows. Sometimes the path is riddled with obstacles; other times it's clear and easy. You're elated to find a fun adventure partner, but then you take different paths. Sometimes that is a blessing; sometimes it's deflating.

You're tempted along the way to sit on a rock and just be present to where you've come and where you are. The perspective may be a beautiful vista, highlighting how far you've progressed. Or it could be depressing to see the distance you've trudged and not glimpse the end yet.

But you know to stay stagnant would not garner the future you envision and long for. So you give yourself a pep talk and keep trekking. You remind yourself to enjoy the journey and notice the beauty and uniqueness of everything — and everyone — you encounter, even though it may not look fetching at the time. You remind yourself that all of life has some lesson and ultimate good, if you are willing to look for it.

So you ignore the pressure to take the media's Valentine's Day messages to mean you are defective if you don't have a sweetheart right now. You can use the barrage of candy, flower and jewelry ads to remind yourself that true love begins with your being besotted with yourself. Try wooing yourself during this time of year and do things that rekindle your infatuation with the person who is key to allowing anyone else to adore you — that would be you!

And you keep on your path, with a renewed verve and oozing love from your core. Your ardor for yourself will attract the right partner to dance down the path of life.

Is he selling too hard?

"**Y**ou'll never meet another guy like me" he said confidently during our first phone call.

I refrained from saying "Duh. Everyone's unique," but I decided it would be better to play along. I wanted to see what he thought was unique. "How so?" I asked, curious about what he'd say.

"How many men have you met who retired at 44?" said the 51-year-old, 27-year military veteran.

"A few," I said truthfully.

"How many men have you met who have no children around, no drama from ex-wives and no money issues?"

"Not many," I replied, feeling I should throw him a bone.

"I'm healthy, STD-free, and work out regularly. I can do whatever I want when I want."

"You are a rarity," I cooed, now clear he was seeking acknowledgement.

But why was he selling himself so hard? We'd already laughed and seemed to be getting along nicely. Did he feel he had to convince me to have coffee with him? I didn't feel there was a need for a sales job.

I realize I can be intimidating to a lot of men, so I've learned to be nice and as gracious as I can. I don't want to be intimidating, but I find many men are not used to talking to an articulate, focused, present woman. So I try to put them at ease and give them some slack so they don't have to try to impress me on the first call.

When people try a bit too hard it backfires. They want to impress you, but by trying to do so they actually seem needy and less confident than they are intending.

Does overselling indicate someone is compensating? Often. They don't realize that others are actually more impressed by how someone treats them and behaves around them than by being told what a terrific person they are.

Have you been on the receiving end of someone trying too hard? Have you ever found yourself trying a bit too much?

Get your bad self on

o you know how to feel sexy?

This seems like an odd question for someone in midlife. But an attractive, midlife woman came up to me after I gave a talk at an executive women's event where she modeled in the fashion show.

"That was a very cute dress you modeled." I shared when she came to shake my hand.

"Are you going to buy it?"

"No, no. It's not really me," she responded.

"It was sexy on you showing your cute figure."

"I just can't see wearing it anywhere."

"Really? Not on a date night with a special someone?"

"Funny you say that. I'm 47 and have been divorced for a few years and my 20-year-old daughter says I should start dating."

"Do you feel ready?"

"I want to have someone special in my life, but I'm not sure I know how to be sexy. You see, I'm a financial analyst and sit with a bunch of nerdy guys all day. I'd never wear anything form-fitting to work."

"It's probably not appropriate to do so at work. But after work, get your bad self on!"

"I don't really know how to do that."

"If you bought that dress — and I have no relationship with those selling it — I bet you'd find a place to wear it. Maybe out for drinks with gal pals at first. Then when you start dating, it would be perfect for dinner with a great guy. But if you don't have anything fun and flirty in your closet, it will be hard to get used to wearing something that shows off your assets."

"I don't mind showing my legs. But not my arms."

"You've got great legs. And that dress was short enough to showcase them while still being age-appropriate. You don't have to have bare arms if you don't want to."

"It's a bit of a stretch to wear something sexy."

"Stretching is good. It can't be too much or you'll never wear the dress. But a little stretching is a great way to grow."

"Thanks. I think I'll get the dress and find a place to wear it."

"You go girl! Get your bad self on!"

What do you know you could do to stretch yourself to be and feel a bit sexier?

Do you see yourself as others see you?

Various studies have shown that few people see themselves as others see them. We tend to either over-rate or underrate our attractiveness compared to others' collective rating of us.

How is it that you can look in the mirror and say, "Looking good!" and others think you need help. I've recently decided our self-view is anything but reliable. A date snapped a pic of me in what I thought was a cute, flattering outfit. The pic he sent me didn't reflect what I thought was my cuteness. "Maybe it was the angle or lighting," I told myself.

Maybe not.

Recently, I've been going through a crisis about my appearance. A few months ago, I had my professional portrait taken at a hefty expense. I liked the pics, as did many colleagues, friends and clients. People commented on how much they liked my hair, which, after decades of struggle, I've finally decided I like long and straight, but with a curl on the end. I've even had strangers stop me to tell me how beautiful my hair is. "Aha," I thought, "I finally have a style that works!"

Then a few months ago, a dear friend said, "I'd love to see what they'd do for you on one of those make-over shows." "What????!!!" I inwardly screamed. "She thinks I need a make over?" She added, "I'd love to see what they'd do with your hair so it is more flattering and less Morticia-like."

Arrgh!

Then I sent some recent video footage to my video producer. He liked the content, but said, "You need a new hair style. It looks outdated and matronly." He even put his wife, a former hair stylist and makeup artist, on the phone to explain to me what she thought was the problem and how it could be fixed.

Arrgh again!

I worked to listen to each of these advisors, as I know they have my best interest at heart. They were not trying to be mean or hurtful. So I listened with that orientation.

The final straw came when I was having my hair and makeup done by a stylist at a talk I was giving. He didn't know me, but I wanted an unbiased opinion. I told him what my video producer and friend had said, and he agreed that my hair could be more flattering.

While I generally believe in trusting one's instincts and being true to yourself, sometimes you don't do yourself any favors by insisting on sticking to something that you like but isn't serving you well. So while I've gotten lots of compliments — something that didn't happen until recently — I've decided to go for a change. I have an appointment with the hair stylist my image consultant recommended. I have my fingers crossed that she'll do her magic.

The lesson for me is that I don't think I have a good lens to see myself as others do. And I doubt many of us do.

Have you had trusted friends or advisers give you feedback that is counter to your own perception? If enough of them do, then put your own aside and take theirs. Our lens is skewed.

Crown of glory

H air.

It can either be a source of pride or vexation. Women typically either love or hate their manes. If a woman's tresses behave as she desires, she's very happy. If not, she bemoans her bad hair genes. Sometimes both in the same day.

What does a woman's hair have to do with dating? A lot, it seems.

How a woman feels about her hair before a date influences her self-image. This affects how she behaves on a date. If she's having a bad hair day, she doesn't feel attractive, which impacts her confidence. She doesn't feel she's putting her best foot (hair) forward.

If she likes her hair that day, she has a spring in her step, a smile on her face, an isn't-life-grand attitude.

The style of her hair matters, too. If she has a wash-and-wear cut, she can spontaneously say yes to a walk in the rain or a swim in the lake. However, if she knows it will take hours to craft her locks into something she considers presentable, she's likely to pass on that convertible ride, no matter how cute the driver. (A gal pal was an hour late for a set-time dinner party because she was doing her hair!)

Some women manage bad hair days with hats, scarves and barrettes. As long as it's attractive, great. But some seem to lean on these accessories rather than try to wrangle their mop into something more appealing. A midlife pal with thin, limp hair has taken to plopping on an unattractive hat when attending professional events. She doesn't want to take the time to learn how to style it to be more becoming.

Semi-permanent solutions play into the mix. The amount we spend on braids, weaves, extensions and dye is staggering. Comedian Chris Rock explores the societal complexities of African-Americans' hair habits in his insightful and hilarious documentary film, "Good Hair." Rock says, "I knew women wanted to be beautiful, but I didn't know the lengths they would go to, the time they would spend — and not complain about it." Beauty, as we all know, is in the eye of the one holding the blow dryer (or paying someone to do it for them).

At some point we had to decide (or perhaps are still deciding), "Should we color or not?" This decision has many ramifications including how one perceives herself, how she wants to be perceived, whether she feels pressured to do something she really doesn't want to do. If she decides to dye, can she afford to have a professional do it or can she do it herself? Should she stick to her natural color or use this as an opportunity to explore something different? Or perhaps straddle the fence and go for a frosted look that plays up some gray? Or maybe let it go au natural and let whatever nature intended be seen?

Hair length is pondered, too, not only for ease of maintenance (or lack thereof) and how it balances one's face and body, but for how one is perceived by potential suitors. While lots of women look sexy in short-cropped or even bald heads, I've been surprised by the number of men's online profiles that say their ideal match has long hair. The age-range of these men's desired match isn't younger women, as I'd assumed, but midlife women. However, midlife women with below-the-shoulder coifs aren't that common.

One man told me that he pre-determines a woman's libido by her hair length. He said below the shoulder meant she was frisky. Between the shoulder and ear, still interested. Above the ear — couldn't care less about the horizontal tango. I'd never heard anything like this, and many short-styled women tell me he is completely wrong. Yet it made me wonder how many men had a similar imaginary passion indicator.

For myself, I left my locks natural until 10 years ago. I liked the salt-and pepper look until three things happened:

💚 the salt began to overtake the pepper;

💚 I felt I looked older than I felt; and

💚 someone guessed my age at many years older than my actual age.

So vanity and a desire to look as young as I felt motivated me to spend many hours and untold dollars in a colorist's care.

My hair is below the shoulder, having previously spent a decade with Rod Stewart-length hair. I never really liked the look, and each time I visited my stylist I told her I felt better about myself when I had some curl in my hair. Yet I'd leave her chair with gelled spikes on the top, which I'd go home and wash out. Because I have a lot of thick, coarse hair, I stupidly returned thinking she was one of the rare stylists who knew how to work with my mop. One day, at home after a styling, I cried when I looked in the mirror, so vowed never to return. I'm clear on what image makes me feel the best about myself. However, my stylist has orders to whack off a few inches when I begin to look like those middle-aged women trying to pass for 30.

How do you feel about your hair and how it affects your sense of attractiveness? How have men reacted to your hair? Has a sweetie ever influenced you to do something different with your hair?

Resources

Make sure to download your free eBook Attract Your Next Great Mate: Dating Advice From Top Relationship Experts at www.DatingGoddess. com/freebie

Afterword

At the time of this writing, I have not yet found my true King Charming. I continue my search with verve. I've become more discerning about what I want and don't want. I've met some wonderful men pals — my treasures — who continue to be in touch.

I wish you much luck in your adventure. It will be fun and frustrating, exhilarating and exasperating, and sexy or sexless. So much depends on you, your approach and your attitude. My books are designed to help you enjoy as much as possible and ward off unpleasantness. But nearly all adventures have wonderful highs as well as a few lows. If you know that going in and arm yourself with information on what to expect, you'll have more of the positives and fewer of the negatives.

Please drop by www.DatingGoddess.com and join in the discussion and report on your experiences.

Dating Goddess

Resources

Go to www.datinggoddess.com to access a variety of useful resources. We work to suggest resources we think have value.

Dating and relationship book reviews

These reviews will save you time and money as I've given you my take on specific books, CDs and more. Some are worth your effort to buy and read or listen to them — some are not. We're always adding new book reviews, so check frequently. We'll also notify our mailing list when new resources are added.

Dating site links

There are a lot of dating sites on the Internet. I've listed the ones I think are worth investigating.

Dating products and tools

Dating can be daunting. We're continually looking at

ways to make it easier and more fun. We'll provide info on games, tools, even date-wear that will help others know you're available, or help you get to know potential suitors better.

Dating and relationship advice sites

Advice "experts" abound on the Internet as anyone can self-proclaim themseves as expert — even if they haven't dted in 30 years and never in midlife. I've worked to find experts who's advice I generally think is solid.

Midlife recources

We'll feature Web sites, books, events and other resources we think might interest you.

Newly discovered resources

I'll add other resources as we discover them, subscribe to our mailing list to get the scoop as soon as we find them. Go to www.DatingGoddess.com to register for our mailing list. Don't worry, we won't sell or give your email to anyone.

Acknowledgments

Let me start by acknowledging the 112 men who helped trigger the lessons contained in this book. Some prompted several! They remain nameless here to protect their identity, although most would recognize references to them. Plus the thousands more whose winks, emails and calls didn't result in a date, but helped me learn the dating game. And all those men who I emailed who never responded — such a blessing to have them weed themselves out.

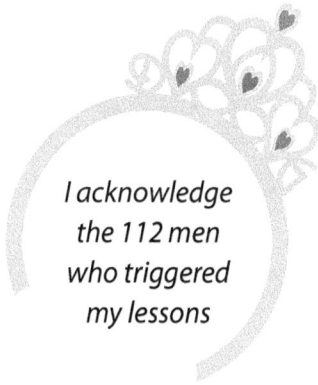

> I acknowledge the 112 men who triggered my lessons

I'd like to thank my Seven Sisters mastermind group for the tremendous brainstorming, noodling, strategizing and encouragement. I wouldn't have begun this project without the prodding of Val Cade, Chris Clarke-Epstein, Mariah Burton Nelson, Sue Dyer, Sam Horn and Marilynn Mobley.

Thank you to my good friends who've listened to my dating stories ad nauseam, and whose support and wisdom are embedded in this text. Ed Betts, Ken Braly, Bruce Daley, Tom Drews, Elaine Floyd, Paulette Ensign, Scott Friedman, Mary Jansen, Tom Johnson, Sandy Jones, Ellie Klevins, Mary Kilkenny, Patrick Lynch, Mary Marcdante, Barbara McNichol, Ann Peterson, Anthony Ramsey, Kristy Rogers, Caterina Rando, Jana Stanfield, Holly Steil, Terry Tepliz, and George Walther, thank you.

The Adventures in Delicious Dating After 40 series

The *Adventures in Delicious Dating After 40* series is designed to help you understand your own midlife dating journey. It is not a road map, as we all take different routes. It is a guide to help you understand yourself, midlife men, and the dating process. Hopefully, you'll not only learn from the lessons and insights shared in this series, but you'll examine how they apply — or don't — to your own dating adventure.

You'll get the scoop on what you need to know, what's changed since you last dated, and how to navigate inevitable bumps in the road.

Following is an overview of each book in the series and a sampling of some of the chapter titles. All are detailed at www.DatingGoddess.com.

Date or Wait: Are You Ready for Mr. Great?

Are you ready for a special man in your life? You have a great life. But you know you'd like a special man to share it. You think you're ready to date, but you haven't done it in a while.

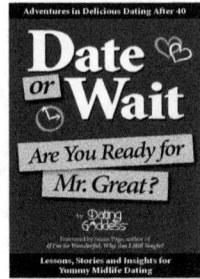

What should you consider before you actually start dating full bore? Even if you've reentered the dating world, this will give you a foundation of attitude and philosophy to make your adventure more fulfilling.

Sample chapters

💜 From hurt to flirt

💜 Dating is like Baskin-Robbins

💜 You've got to kiss a lot of…princes!

💜 What's your definition of dating success?

💜 Are you open to receiving?

💜 Dating: A self-designed personal-growth workshop

💜 Hands-on dating research

💜 Being present to the presents

💜 Being aggressively single

💜 Approaching dating like a buffet

💜 Is Brad Pitt ruining your love life?

💜 Treasures can come in dented packages

Assessing Your Assets: Why You're A Great Catch

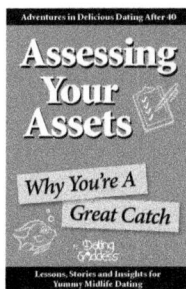

You have many wonderful qualities. But it's easy to focus on one's flaws — at least what seem like flaws to you. However, to the right man your imperfections are endearing, attractive and lovable. You have to be clear what you offer a man who will find you enchanting.

Assessing Your Assets helps you look at what you bring to a new relationship. It will help you see your good points so you'll approach dating with more confidence.

Sample chapters

🖤 Don't think you are damaged goods

🖤 You are (probably) more attractive than you think!

🖤 They aren't called "hate handles"

🖤 Are you a good man picker?

🖤 What are your deal breakers?

🖤 Are you arguing your limitations?

🖤 Turn your liabilities into assets

🖤 The strong vs. nice woman debate

🖤 Is your sense of humor stunting your dating?

🖤 Why are we drawn to bad boys?

🖤 The zest test

In Search of King Charming: Who Do I Want to Share My Throne?

You are no longer looking for "Prince" Charming because you are a queen. You want someone who is at your level, not groveling at your feet. You want a king — someone who's your equal and with whom you can rule the throne together!

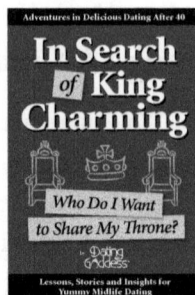

This book focuses on helping you better define what you want beyond tall, dark and handsome! You'll consider characteristics you might not have thought of before. You'll look at what you want now.

Sample chapters

💚 Building your Franken-boyfriend

💚 What's your "perfect boyfriend's" job description?

💚 A man to go with your wardrobe

💚 In search of the elusive good kisser

💚 When you're clear on what you want, it appears

💚 Are you dating the same guy in different bodies?

💚 Does he fit in your world?

💚 What's your kissing quotient?

💚 Is your guy's loving muscle strong?

💚 Do you both have the same dating rhythm?

Embracing Midlife Men: Insights Into Curious Behaviors

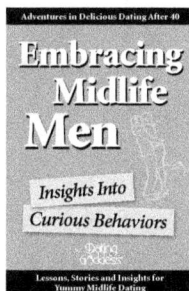

Do you sometimes scratch your head after interacting with a midlife man, wondering, "What could he possibly be thinking?" Especially if it's before, during or after a date with a man who presumably wants to impress you!

This book focuses on better understanding midlife men's behaviors. When you grasp what's going on in his head it's much easier to embrace him. Men are wondrous creatures, so we need to understand them better and love them for who they are.

Sample chapters

💜 Men are like shoes

💜 Why men disappear when it gets serious

💜 Chivalry isn't dead —but it seems to be hibernating

💜 Do men want feisty women?

💜 Midlife men have forgotten how to date

💜 Are you getting prime time from your man?

💜 When a man tells you what he paid for things

💜 Does he treat you like his ex?

💜 Has Greg Behrendt done women a disservice?

💜 Tales of woo

Dipping Your Toe in the Dating Pool: Dive In Without Belly Flopping

You've decided you are ready — you want to start dating. Maybe you've already had a few coffee dates with several men. You want to be as successful as possible on your dating adventure.

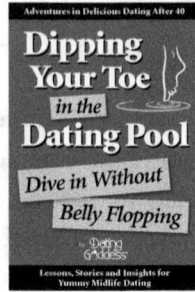

This book focuses on getting started on your dating adventures. We cover what you need to know as you begin your journey.

Sample chapters

💜 Do you have the right datewear?

💜 Dating with integrity

💜 Building your rejection muscle

💜 When "be yourself" is questionable advice

💜 Faux beaus and practice dating

💜 Are you making bad decisions out of loneliness?

💜 Being "in wonder" about your date's behavior

💜 When do you feel most vulnerable in dating?

💜 Are you out of his league — or he yours?

💜 Why listening is so seductive

Winning at the Online Dating Game: Stack the Deck in Your Favor

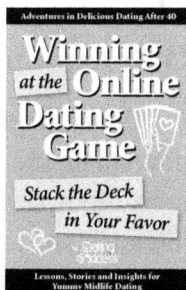

Internet dating can be frustrating or fruitful. It will be much less exasperating if you know how to read and weed out men's profiles that aren't appropriate for you. And you'll have a steady stream of potential suitors if you know how to write a compelling profile for yourself.

This book focuses on the ins and outs of online dating. How to play the game, which has it's own rules and language. If you don't understand how online dating works, you'll waste a lot of time connecting with men who are not a possible fit for you.

Sample chapters

💜 Shopping for men

💜 Safe online dating

💜 Is 21st Century dating unnatural?

💜 What do men look at in your profile?

💜 Euphemisms uncovered

💜 Are you describing yourself compellingly?

💜 No, I will not be dating your Harley

💜 Playing the online dating game

💜 Scantily clothed pictures

Check Him Out Before Going Out: Avoiding Dud Dates

Under the cloak of the anonymity that email and the phone provides, men often reveal more than they intend. If you ask the right questions you can find out a lot about his values and view of the world after just an interaction or two.

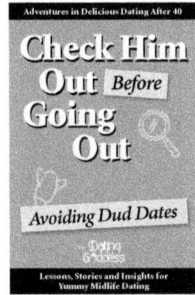

This book focuses on what you need to ask before agreeing to even a coffee date. You need to vet the men who email and call you to ensure you're not likely to waste your time with men who clearly aren't a match.

Sample chapters

💜 Becoming smitten with the fantasy

💜 Can Google help — or hinder — your dating life?

💜 Qualify your potential dates before meeting

💜 The art of consideration

💜 Anticipating a big date is like awaiting Santa

💜 Being seduced by what he is over who he is

💜 Are you his spare?

💜 My boyfriend, whom I haven't met

💜 When canceling is the right thing to do

💜 Politics, religion and sex — oh my!

First-Rate First Dates: Increasing the Chances of a Second Date

You can tell a lot about someone within the first 30 minutes. What does he talk about? Does he ask you questions? If so, what does he want to know about you? What do you need to know about him? How does he treat you? How does he treat those around you?

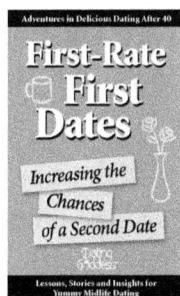

This book focuses on what goes on during the first date. How do you determine if you want a second date? What you can do to increase the likelihood your date will ask you for a second? That is if you want a repeat!

Sample chapters

💜 Start with coffee

💜 How do you greet him?

💜 When it clicks, throw out some of your criteria

💜 Tracking your date's score

💜 Clues a guy is just looking for a booty call

💜 12 signs he won't be asking for a second date

💜 First-date red flags that this guy isn't for you

💜 Honesty is not always the best policy

💜 Chemistry, or does he make my toes curl?

💜 Women's first-date blunders

Real Deal or Faux Beau: Should You Keep Seeing Him?

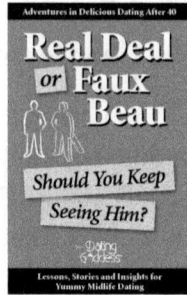

Adventures in Delicious Dating After 40

Real Deal *or* **Faux Beau**

Should You Keep Seeing Him?

Lessons, Stories and Insights for Yummy Midlife Dating

You've begun to go out with a man you like. How do you decide if you should continue seeing him, or if you should release him because he's not The One?

This book focuses on second dates and beyond. During the dating process you are both assessing if you want to keep seeing each other. This book helps you determine what questions you need to ask yourself.

Sample chapters

💜 Deciding to see him again or not

💜 What's your date's Delight/Disappointment Scale score?

💜 Broaching tough conversations

💜 "I want to respect me in the morning"

💜 Does he invite you to his place?

💜 Are you stingy in dating?

💜 When his hand is on your knee too soon

💜 Easy way to ask hard questions

💜 Rose-colored glasses obscure red flags

💜 If his stories don't add up, subtract yourself

Multidating Responsibly: Play the Field Without Being A Player

Playing the field is frowned on in some circles. There are definitely appropriate and inappropriate ways to date several men simultaneously.

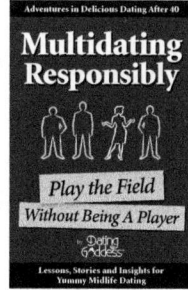

This book focuses on how to date around responsibly and with integrity without leading men on. If you do it with honesty, you can date several people at once until you're both ready to focus only on each other.

Sample chapters

💚 "Pimpin'" — Dating multiple guys

💚 Multi-dating pros and cons

💚 Your Date-A-Base — tracking multiple suitors

💚 "Hot bunking" your beaus

💚 Are you a "Let's Make a Deal" type of dater?

💚 Assume there are other women

💚 Dating's revolving door

💚 How long do you hedge your bet?

💚 Beware of multi-tasking when multi-dating

💚 Back burner beaus

💚 The boyfriend phone

Moving On Gracefully: Break Up Without Heartache

"Breaking up" sounds so high school, doesn't it? But part of the dating process is saying something when one of you decides not to date the other anymore. Going "poof" is not a mature or respectful option in midlife.

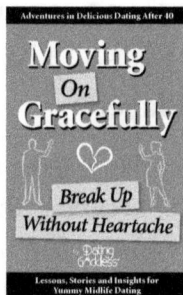

This book focuses on surviving a breakup, whether you initiate it or not. Either way, it's never easy to break up if you have developed any fondness toward the other.

Sample chapters

💚 Hello — goodbye: How to say no thanks after meeting

💚 Releasing back into the dating pool

💚 50 ways to leave your lover? 4 ways not to leave your suitor

💚 Breaking up is hard to do — right

💚 Why men go "poof"

💚 How to trump being dumped

💚 When breaking up is a "Get Out of Jail Free" card

💚 How to detect the end is near

💚 Failed relationships' blessings

💚 He's broken up with you — he just didn't tell you

💚 Rejection is protection

From Fear to Frolic: Get Naked Without Getting Embarrassed

This book focuses on what you need to consider and know before getting physically intimate with a man you're dating. This is nerve-wracking to many midlife women. This book will prepare you.

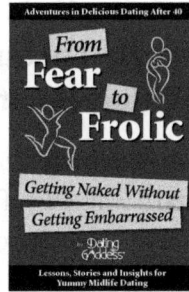

Sample chapters

💜 Sleepover do's and don'ts

💜 Does he want in your life — or just in your bedroom?

💜 Getting naked with him the first time

💜 An excuse to seduce or how important is bedroom bliss?

💜 What to ask yourself before getting naked with him

💜 Are you and your guy on the same sexual time line?

💜 Sharing your sexual owner's manual with him

💜 What women need from a man before having sex

💜 Why too-soon midlife sex is like non-fat food

💜 How dating sex is like waffles

💜 Too-soon seduction: "I'm special, but not THAT special"

Ironing Out Dating Wrinkles: Work Through Challenges Without Getting Steamed

Nearly all relationships have some ups and downs. Part of getting to know someone is knowing how they work through relationship misunderstandings.

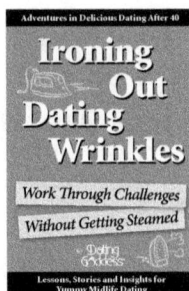

This book focuses on how to work through the inevitable hiccups that happen when you are getting to know each other. If you can both deal with challenges, the bond deepens and you find yourself smitten.

Sample chapters

💜 When your guy vexes you, ask what your highest self would do

💜 The first fight

💜 You want boo; he wants boo-ty

💜 Where's the line between getting your needs met and being selfish?

💜 Expressing your upset with your guy

💜 Is his toothbrush in your cabinet too soon?

💜 Do you love how he loves you?

💜 Is he collecting data on how to make you happy?

💜 Be careful of being smitten

💜 Exclusivity: How and when to broach it